The Hungry Sheep

BOOKS BY JOHN D. SHERIDAN

Essays

I Can't Help Laughing
I Laugh to Think
Half in Earnest
My Hat Blew Off
The Right Time
While the Humour Is on Me
Funnily Enough
Bright Intervals
Joking Apart
Include Me Out

Novels

Paradise Alley
The Magnificent MacDarney
The Rest Is Silence
God Made Little Apples
Vanishing Spring
Here's Their Memory

Poetry

Joe's No Saint
Stirabout Lane

JOHN D. SHERIDAN

The Hungry Sheep

Catholic Doctrine Restated
Against Contemporary Attacks

ARLINGTON HOUSE·PUBLISHERS
NEW ROCHELLE, N. Y.

NIHIL OBSTAT: Cathaldus McCarthy

IMPRIMI POTEST: Dermitius,
     ✠ Archiep. Dublinen., Hiberniae Primas

die 8a augusti, 1973

Library of Congress Catalog Card Number:73–17003

MANUFACTURED IN THE UNITED STATES OF AMERICA

Library of Congress Cataloging in Publication Data

Sheridan, John Desmond, 1903–
    The hungry sheep.

    Includes bibliographical references.
    1. Catholic Church--Apologetic works. I. Title.
BX1752.S53   230'.2   73-17003
ISBN 0-87000-265-1

Contents

The hungry sheep look up and are not fed.
                                        —*Lycidas*

Foreword

This book has been a long time in the making. In a sense it began forty years ago when I showed Frank O'Connor the manuscript of my first novel. His verdict was not encouraging (though he softened it a little by saying that my eye was as good as his own), and he recognised the attempt for what it really was—a sort of literary Czerny exercise. (I had wanted to write *something,* and a novel seemed as good a bet as the next.) The long and the short of it was, he said—or words to that effect—that I had no story to tell.

Then he closed his eyes, leaned back, and said that it was all but impossible for a Catholic to write a good novel. A novelist must deal with crises, must resolve human problems in human terms, and the Catholic was constantly bumping against the walls of dogma. Tethered and spancelled, he was cut off from the free speculation which is the stuff of drama.

I was more impressed by the instrument than by the tune (which was one on which O'Connor was to play endless variations), for he had a wonderful voice and the rich overtones in his soft Cork vowels barely stopped short of being diphthongs, but though I sensed the flaw in his reasoning I did not do well in the discussion that followed. After all, I was a mere junior, and he was on the point of taking silk. Moreover, he had done me a favour in reading my manuscript, and I was at something of a disadvantage.

But the truth—as I saw dimly then and was to see more clearly afterwards—is that it is not the Catholic who is hampered in speculation but the man who, unfettered by dogma, is free to go where he pleases. It is only when one *does* bump one's head against a wall that one has to rub it and think things out. If there are no walls and no bumps there is no mental enlargement—and very little fun. If there is only one exit from the maze the joy of finding it makes up for the frustration of going round in circles.

Dogma gives the answers, but it leaves us to do our own homework, and we have to begin all over again every time we take a wrong turning. The Catholic, as Arnold Lunn says, is the real rationalist. He must give reasons for the faith that is in him, and this is a duty which he owes not only to himself and his neighbour but also to God almighty; for it is scant courtesy to the God who has equipped us with minds if we confine our speculations to physics, astronomy, and the mechanics of the golf swing and fail to nibble occasionally at philosophy and theology—which are the most fascinating of all studies, since they not only help to place us in our proper relation to Him but reveal us more fully to ourselves.

Moreover, some attempt to survey the intellectual basis of faith is necessary for its buttressing. Simple faith is all very well, but it takes a heavy battering in days when attacks come from within the Church as well as from without, and when so many priests and prelates, under the pretext of updating the Church, are challenging basic truths, flouting the authority of the Magisterium, flirting openly with Marxism, and putting their trust in evolution, progress, and other strange gods.

So if my interview with Frank O'Connor marked the beginning of this book as a vague and formless idea it was the sequel to Vatican II which forced me after almost a lifetime of postponements to get down finally to the writing of it; especially as the grain of truth in the quip that the theme song of the Council was "Should old Aquinas be forgot?" has sprouted alarmingly since.

8

Aquinas, of course, even at the best of times, was for the few. He makes every objection seem unanswerable until he demolishes it; he is so tersely logical that the spark of reason has to cross wide synapses at times, and not every dynamo is tuned for the job. Küng, Haring, and Schillebeeckx are easier going, not just because they fall far short of his intellectual stature but also because, thanks to the mass media and what used to be the Catholic press, their statements are neatly capsuled and passed on to the general public. The result is that the man in the street, who in the days when the Church spoke with one voice might have got official rulings by knocking at any presbytery, is utterly confused on such issues as papal infallibility, freedom of conscience (every man his own theologian), and "co-responsibility." Young priests in polo-neck sweaters (and old ones who should know better) tell him that things are managed more democratically in Holland, advise him to read Teilhard de Chardin (though the Monitum of the Sacred Congregation on the dangers of Teilhard's "theology-fiction," as Maritain calls it, is still in force), and bewilder him by saying that he need not worry unduly about his own inner spiritual life so long as he loves his neighbour and is concerned about starvation in the Third World.

He is told too that before the Council no one participated fully in the Mass (which makes him recall how well his grandmother got by with her beads), and he feels so alien in churches where the altar has become a table, where the tabernacle is hidden away (lest it should be a barrier to ecumenism), and where participation is measured in decibels, that he has difficulty in convincing himself that he is still in his Father's house. He usually reacts in one or other of two ways: he carries on, trusting that things will come right in the end, or he makes his own protest and has things out once in a while with priests who seem to be teaching near-heresies and with nuns who send his children home with the glad tidings that Adam is a biblical myth and that the new theologians will

9

soon come up with an aseptic explanation of what used to be called original sin.

If he chooses the latter course he need not feel abashed or tongue-tied because he has had no formal training in philosophy or theology, for he still has the answer book which so many who have failed to profit by such a training seem to have mislaid. The teaching of the Magisterium can be his guide, and he need have no qualms about challenging anything which clashes with it. For the deposit of faith is unchanged and unchangeable; the walls of dogma are still standing, and as ever their astringent and comforting reality is the infallible antidote and answer to wrong thinking.

It would be presumptuous of me to describe this book as a refresher course in apologetics (though that is a fair enough description of what the writing of it involved), but never was it more necessary for Catholics not only to brief themselves anew on basic dogmas (and the timing of the *Credo* of Pope Paul, which was addressed to the people rather than to the prelates, is proof that we live in days of challenge and crisis) but also to survey for themselves the solid intellectual basis on which their faith rests. No one may stand aside, and the layman least of all.

The main reason for the decline of Christianity in the modern world, writes Arnold Lunn in *Unkilled for So Long*, is loss of nerve, and he quotes the distinguished Anglican, Professor E. L. Mascall, as saying that it is this failure which has "stampeded so many contemporary theologians into a total capitulation to their secular environment." When there has been so calamitous a decline in morale amongst churchmen it behooves the laity to stand firm, and digging our feet in involves not only courage and loyalty but a review of the Church's title deeds.

I
A Starting Point

"Human thought," says Pope Paul VI, "aims not only at knowing things but also at discovering the whys and wherefores, the essential causes of the things themselves . . . It is the supreme torment of intelligence, the religious torment . . . For thinking man to pass from agnostic or atheistic ignorance to recognition of a necessary natural religion is a difficult process." *

As Catholics, we are spared much of the torment, since we can recite the Creed and take the rest on trust. But something more is expected of us. Our faith must have a rational basis, and our belief—not only our belief in the Church but in the existence of God—is the stronger for some examination of the whys and the wherefores. We must start from scratch, like the philosophers, lacking their capacity for thinking at this level but following their footsteps on the road they have signposted.

I begin with myself. I look out and see otherness, and it is this otherness, even before I begin to sort and label it (and when I was an infant the sorting was a long and cumulative process) which makes me aware of the self. When I bump against things, either physically or by realising their separateness, I become conscious of the fact that there are things that bump and something against which they bump. I look out at things which have objective exis-

*General audience, 12 Jan., 1972

11

tence and are not merely projections of my own subjective ideas. I become conscious of the Me and the Not Me.

But how do I know things other than myself? What is the relation between the knower and the thing known in the very act of knowing? There must be a link, a junction, a bridging point. Knowing, the philosophers say, is *becoming*. I do not become a flower when I observe its shape and colouring and speculate on the disposition of its parts, but I am changed for ever after. I have taken in something. I have grasped it in a double sense. There is a commerce—to my profit—between the Me and the Not Me, and I am not a prisoner of the self.

Impressions come to me through my senses, but there is something which uses these impressions as raw material for absorption, as the data for that mysterious activity which we call thought. Is this something a part or function of my material body? Obviously it is free from the limitations of my material body. It can project itself to the stars and back or to the days of the Roman legions in the twinkling of an eye; and this instancy, this independence of time and space is not a property of material things, which are either here or there, but not both, and which take time to move from one to the other.

This something within me (and yet not within, in the localized sense that my liver and kidneys are within me) not only receives messages and decodes and edits them but in a very real sense is at both ends of the line. A tingling at the end of my finger is a physical sensation, but that which adverts to it and ponders on its cause is in two places at once—in the tingling area and in the control station which adverts to the tingling, locates it, and reflects on it. And if it is not localized, how can it be material?

The brain is certainly involved—this mass of greyish-white matter which I carry under my hat—but only as a subsidiary, for the brain is a material thing, with vast ganglia of feeder lines and communications, and millions of tiny cells. Is there a master-cell

12

which has the power of producing that non-material thing called thought? If there is, we must go further in our search, for every cell has its components, and if we are looking for the man in charge we are faced with a problem in unending diminution.

Moreover, since thought is non-material, its agent must be non-material; there must be a correspondence between subject and object. Here, parting company with the materialists, we speak first of a soul and then of a spiritual soul. Every living thing has a soul (which is what makes a stone different from a daisy, and a live worm different from a dead one), but man alone has a spiritual soul.

A spirit has no parts and occupies no space (which gets rid of the problem of unending diminution), but whilst this is easy to say it is hard to grasp; hard to grasp and impossible to *imagine;* for when we try to imagine something which has no parts and occupies no space we conjure up a non-picture of nothingness. It is difficult for us to do otherwise, for we are accustomed to think of everything as having size and occupying space—attributes which are common to ourselves, the elephant, and the atom. But if the concept of spirit is difficult (and it undoubtedly *is* difficult) we must remember that our own thoughts, the reality of which we never doubt, have something in common with spirit, since they too cannot be weighed or measured and occupy no space. Talking of size or extension with regard to spirit is like talking of weight or colour with regard to a trumpet note. The terms do not apply.

The materialist, rejecting the notion of a spiritual soul because it is unimaginable (though it is not inconceivable), sees the brain as the origin and explanation of thought. The brain obviously plays an important part in our thinking, but if there were no non-material component to collate and interpret the information reaching it, the brain would have no more significance than a computer working on blindly in a city where nuclear fallout has killed all the inhabitants.

Psychologists and surgeons have established that certain operations and functions are associated with certain lobes of the brain, but this knowledge tells us nothing about the intellect, any more than the knowledge that messages from a particular suburb are handled in a particular part of the city telephone exchange can tell us anything of the messages themselves or of the people who send them. It enables surgeons to locate clots that have brought about local paralysis, but no neuromuscular blueprint of the brain's complex communication lines can explain or account for the phenomenon of thought.

The brain can no more weigh premises and reach conclusions than the eye can really see. The physical eye provides the necessary equipment (necessary, because the soul acts in and through and with the co-operation of the body)—the muscles which bring the image into focus, the screen on which it flashes—but "seeing," in the wider sense, pertains to the soul. There is no power in veined jelly to sift and interpret, and there is a very real sense in which it can be said that every ear is deaf and every eye stone blind.

What is it in us, Pascal asks, that feels pleasure?* Is it the hand, the arm, the flesh, the blood? Or is it, he might have continued, the grey mass of the brain or the nerves that supply its multitudinous cells? Thoughts, ideas, questions of how, whence, and why —these are not material things, and that which judges, thinks, takes counsel with itself, accepts or rejects, cannot be laid bare by the surgeon's scalpel, removed like a tumour, or weighed like a duck egg.

One cannot prove the existence of the soul as one proves a geometrical theorem. Nevertheless there are solid philosophical arguments for its existence, and the Greeks thought up some pretty formidable ones more than two thousand years ago. Some early philosophers thought of the body as no more than a prison

*Pensées

14

for the soul. St. Thomas, however, teaches that man is not a spiritualised brute, nor yet an incarnate spirit; neither body nor soul but body-soul.

When I spoke earlier of the spiritual soul as the instrument of thought I was skirting a philosophical difficulty, for that which abstracts, wills, compares, judges, and reaches conclusions is the *compositum*, the body-soul, the *man*. Intelligence is a power of the soul, but the intelligence in action needs the help of the body, since all our ideas without exception (even our idea of spirit) come to us through the senses.

We must not think of a body as being fitted with a soul in much the same way as a car engine is fitted to the next chassis that comes from the production line. In a very real sense of the familiar phrase, my body and my soul were—quite literally—made for one another. My soul, like every spiritual soul, is the form of the body which it animates, and my body is the act of the soul which animates it. When I die, the soul which leaves my body will be no more a man than the bound-for-dissolution thing that it leaves behind.

The soul is immortal, since it has no parts into which it could disintegrate. What then of the body which it animates, and for which it was made, granted that its natural state is to be in that body? To this question, philosophy has no answer. Having said that the soul is immortal, it has nothing to add. It is revelation which tells us that the body will rise again and be reunited with its animating soul, and that their divorce is not forever.

2
More About Myself

Even in my low moments—and I have as many as the next—I realise that I am a wonderful being in that, unlike my dog, I am a *person*. Chicago and roses, symphonies and schnapps, sunsets and the Polar Ice Cap are part of me (knowing is becoming) in a way that fleas and bones and chasing cats can never be a part of him, for he is eternally tethered to his unchanging ration of dogginess. He is what he is as a life sentence. He can know fear and joy, but not remorse or regret. He had an Alsatian and a collie for parents, but he has no knowledge of his lineage. He can never give himself airs, never wonder if he might have done better for himself as a borzoi or a cocker spaniel. He has no ambitions and no dreams.

But I am not tethered. I can cross the Alps with Hannibal or plant a flag on the cold face of the moon. I can luxuriate in my bath and be Chopin or Chaplin as the humour takes me.

The Private Life of Walter Mitty, the story of that lovable character who, plagued by a nagging wife, found comfort in a dream world, is more than a very human story; it is a resumé of the whole human story. But the fantasies of Walt Disney are contradictions of the real animal story; for the real animal story is a short one, and it might be summed up by saying that the cat is always on the mat and the python forever prisoned in the forest.

My glory, and yours, is that each of us is unique. There is nobody

17

else like me, though I have some relatives who, to their own annoyance (and mine) are mistaken for me at times. This annoyance does not spring from pride or vainglory, though it may have traces of both. It is based on an instinctive recognition of the basic theological truth that each of us is unique, a truth which we seldom express explicitly but hide in confessions of faith beginning with "The kind I am" and lists of idiosyncrasies ranging from a passion for tripe and onions to having unusually high insteps.

No two of us are identical, and no one exactly like me, or you, or anyone else, ever walked the earth or ever will walk it.* I cannot be explained, as some psychologists would explain me, solely in terms of heredity and environment. I am *mei generis.*

Heredity certainly played a part in my physical and emotional shaping, and I am indebted to my parents and my lineage for the factors in my genetic formula which determined my racial characteristics, my optimum height, the colour of my hair and the age at which it whitened. Later, the environment got to work on me: the place I lived in, the food I ate, the conversations I heard, the affection, care, and guidance of my parents, the books I read, the social milieu in which I lived. But I was not just something to be moulded and shaped like putty. I was acted upon, undoubtedly, but the mechanism of my shaping was within.

Which brings me to the third and most important factor in my make-up—inexpressibly more important than the others because it makes me the *person* that I am; and also because, its existence being granted, I would have been that same person had I been reared in a completely different environment and born blind. I am a person and unique for one reason and one reason only—because I am animated by a spiritual soul which did not evolve from anything already in existence but was directly created by God.

*We speak of "identical twins", but this is merely a convenient and descriptive biological label. Identical twins are startlingly alike in physical build and temperament. But whatever else they are they are not identical. They are different *persons*, and as such as different one from the other as I am from the man next door.

18

When did I receive my spiritual soul? This is a non-question if ever there was one, since before my soul was created there was no "I" there to receive it. How could there have been, since the "I" is the body-soul, the compositum? Nevertheless the question is asked, though in somewhat different terms, by the abortionists, who quibble amongst themselves (as if they were affected by scruples) regarding the approximate stage of foetal development which must be reached before we can say with reasonable certainty that there is human life in the womb. But life exists from the very moment of conception (a most thrustful and vigorous life at that, with an incredible rate of growth and development), and it must be human life, since the fertilized human ovum never develops into an alligator or a waterhen. And if human life, then a particular human life, since that is the only kind there is—either John Dillinger or John Henry Newman or John Milton. I began—like you and every other mother's son of us—as a fertilized egg. I was body-soul from the instant of my conception, and if that fertilized egg had been stilled early in play or prevented from nidating in the womb towards which it hurried it is I who would have died.

Aquinas, I know, taught differently, saying that the developing human embyro begins with a vegetal soul (like a plant), then acquires a soul that is at once sensitive and vegetal (like that of an animal), and finally a soul that is vegetal, sensitive, and rational. For him, to think of a rational soul in a still unformed embyro was a metaphysical absurdity. But there are two objections to this— apart from the fact that embryology is a much more developed science now than it was in Aquinas's day. The first is that we are concerned with a "human" embyro, and the qualifying adjective loses all meaning if there is no rational soul present. The second may appear naive, but to me it is very convincing, and it is based on a source more authoritative even than Aquinas—the old Penny Catechism. "Christ was always God," it taught, "but He was man only from the time of His conception or incarnation." And if Christ received His created soul at the time of His conception,

19

then surely the question of when human life begins is resolved. (It is significant perhaps that some of the new catechists who reject the second clause of the sentence I have quoted are wobbly also on the first. Once you reject Trent, it would seem, you make a shambles of theology.)

It may be objected that the analogy from Christ's conception has no force, since He was conceived by the Holy Spirit and not in the ordinary way of human generation. But He was truly Man, like to the rest of us in everything but sin, and there was nothing miraculous about His development in His Mother's womb. He was God—and Man—from the instant of His conception. Mary became the Mother of God when she said "Be it done unto me according to Thy word," and she was the temple of the Holy Spirit until her Child was born in Bethlehem.

She herself, too (again the old Catechism can keep us right) "by a tremendous privilege of grace was kept free from the stain of Original Sin." And we have a special name for this privilege. We call it the Immaculate Conception.

3
Men and Monkeys

There was a time when I did not exist; and I could not have been the cause of my own beginning, since that which does not exist cannot bring about its own existence—or anything else for that matter. Obviously I am indebted to someone or something for that existence, not just for my being a man and not a banana or a centipede, but for my being the individual man, the unique compositum of body-soul that I am.

According to the theory of evolution (which as a Catholic I am free to accept with reservations, but which I reject for several reasons, one of them being that it is still an unproven theory, and a very shaky one at that) I am descended from monkeys. My story, as the evolutionists tell it, goes back to the primeval wilderness of ageless time when nothing stirred on the earth. Then, after countless aeons, lifeless matter generated living organisms which throughout a near-eternity grew more and more complex in a variety of groupings and phylums. Fishes grew rudimentary legs (with remarkable foresight and, it would seem, anticipating a use for them in due course); mammals, having learned the trick of breast-feeding their young, went on to perfect their heat-regulating mechanisms; my simian ancestors walked erect, and here I am.

The best-known protagonist of this theory in our own day is the Jesuit, Teilhard de Chardin, whose *Phenomenon of Man*, with its visionary rhapsodies and pseudo-scientific jargon, has acquired

21

such a mystique that those who (like me) find him hard to follow, or who reject as much of him as they can follow, are rated as second-class minds. I make no personal appeal against this verdict, except to point out that Jacques Maritain and Etienne Gilson could be listed on the same charge sheet.

Reading Teilhard I find myself asked to follow a series of unsubstantiated theses—and this apart from the wild fiction of an evolving Christ who will come to full term before the fall of the curtain. The original lifeless matter, Teilhard tells me, generated living forms which moved "through ingenuity" towards "higher psychisms" and improved their quality cumulatively until "hominization occurred" (*occurred* is good) and in the end "thought was born." It is all too easy to be dazzled by the iridescence of his phrasing when he speaks of "directed chance—pervading everything so as to try everything, and trying everything so as to find everything," but the magic soon crumbles. If "directed chance," how directed and by whom? If directed, how chance? And if "ingenuity" is involved, surely this amounts to saying that thought directed and evaluated the probings which resulted eventually in its own birth.

But there is better to come. Searching for my ancestral line, Teilhard rejects the insects because "superior psychic levels demand physically larger brains," dismisses antelopes and elephants because the specialized development of antlers and trunks seems to indicate a "morphological dead end," and after shopping around finds himself left with the primates, noting with approval, and as a point in their favour, their lack of specialized organs tending towards monstrosity.

Having improved the quality of their brains (I wish I could improve the quality of mine), the primates, Teilhard tells us, arrived in due course at "the very frontiers of intelligence" (though there is no such frontier). And in the *The Future of Man* he is even more explicit. "There is nothing," he says, "not even the human soul, that does not come under this universal law . . . the soul must therefore in one way or another have grown out of the general mobility of things." If this is scientific reasoning then the alchemists have been badly maligned. Teilhard is prophet, poet, and seer, but he is no philosopher, and as Father G. H. Duggan says of him: "The ambiguity of his language is matched by the confusion of his thought."*

Teilhard's rating as a scientist has been variously assessed. Sir Alister Hardy says of *The Phenomenon of Man* that, although it is a magnificent epic, it is not a scientific work at all, and Sir Peter Medawar dismissed it as "a high-sounding farrago"; on the other hand, Sir Julian Huxley, who wrote the Introduction to the *Phenomenon*, describes Teilhard as a "distinguished palaeontologist." Huxley's objectivity, however, is open to question, since he says a few paragraphs later that he himself had published an essay in which he independently anticipated the title of Pere Teilhard's great work by describing humanity as a phenomenon, and that he had elsewhere attempted "to relate the development of moral codes and religions to the general trends of evolution." Huxley also says that his own statement to the effect that in modern scientific man evolution "was becoming conscious of itself" had delighted Teilhard, who approved Nietzsche's view that man is unfinished and must be surpassed or completed. There was a close linkage in approach, it would seem, between the agnostic Englishman and the French Jesuit who had obliged by bringing the notion of an evolving Christ into the story of evolution.

Understandably, Huxley does not completely approve. Thus, speaking of Teilhard's Omega point, he writes: "Here his thought is not fully clear to me." Then he goes on: "Sometimes he seems to equate this future hyperpersonal psychosocial organization with an emergent Divinity; at one place, for instance, he speaks of the

Teilhardism and the Faith

trend as *Christogenesis;* and elsewhere he appears not to be guard-
ing himself sufficiently against the danger of personifying the
non-personal elements of reality." But on the charge of Teilhard's
having deviated from the party line, Huxley plumps for honourable
acquittal. "Although many scientists, as I do," he writes, "find it
impossible to follow Teilhard all the way in his gallant attempt to
reconcile the supernatural elements in Christianity with the facts
and implications of evolution, this in no way detracts from the
positive value of his naturalistic general approach."

But the truth is that Teilhard's naturalistic general approach
completely vitiated his attempts—gallant or otherwise—to reconcile the truths of Christianity with the implications of evolution.
If matter and spirit evolve from the same matrix and are but
different forms of the same cosmic stuff, then the attempted
reconciliation is in reality a surrender. As Maritain says of Teilhard: "In his ardent meditation science, faith, mystique, theology
and philosophy are inextricably mingled and confounded, and in
this we are forced to recognise the sin against the intellect—the
refusal to recognise the intrinsic order of the human intelligence."*

(Some years ago, a newly-professed nun to whom I ventured to
open my mind on Teilhard told me coyly that it would be ten years
before "ordinary people" would understand him. So, it appeared,
she had been assured by a theologian who had given the community retreat—and who, it would seem, considered himself no ordinary person. There is some hope for the little nun, but none at all
for me. I shall go to my grave without having seen the light.)

Teilhard, like so many of his disciples amongst latter-day catechists, dismissed Adam as a biblical myth. (John L. McKenzie,
S.J., in his *Dictionary of the Bible,* downgrades the Scriptural
account of Adam's creation from the dust of the earth, saying:

---

* *The Peasant of the Garonne*

24

"The manufacture of man from clay is found both in Egypt and Mesopotamia. The Hebrew account replaces this gross element with the breath of God, the principle of life." The innuendo is clear, and a little later he says: "This account is neither a scientific account of the origin of man nor a history of the beginning of the race in the proper sense of the word.") For Teilhard, man, like every other species, made his first appearence in millions, and our first parents were not only hairy but legion. The first man was a crowd, and his infancy was made up of thousands of years, giving him time to come down out of the trees and speculate on the problem of being. Meanwhile there was a gradual—and praiseworthy—development of cranial shape and size.

The attempts of the evolutionists to adduce evidence in support of their theory make unedifying reading. Bones were dug up, and arguments were based on skulls, jaws, and fragments of teeth. Sometimes, too, there was a little cheating, as in the notorious case of the Piltdown skull (the "discovery" site of which Teilhard visited in 1913). All these were put forward as pieces of the jigsaw puzzle, but the pattern to which they were supposed to conform was arbitrary and pre-determined, and the gaps were so formidable as to rule out acceptance by any but the fanatically committed.

The evolutionists were fully entitled to put forward the theory that all life evolved from lifeless matter, since many advances in human knowledge begin with the inspired guess. What they were not entitled to do was to foist this thesis on the world as a proven fact; but foist it they did—unremittingly, and with remarkable success. Professor W.H.Thompson, a leading British biologist, who was surely qualified to assess the evidence, made a scathing comment on this lack of integrity; and he made it, of all places, in the Introduction which he wrote for the 1965 Dent edition of Darwin's *Origin of Species*. "This situation," he wrote, "where scientific men rally to the defence of a doctrine which they are

25

unable to defend scientifically, much less demonstrate, attempting to maintain its credit with the public by the suppression of criticism and the elimination of difficulties, is abnormal and undesirable in science."

Abnormal and undesirable it certainly was. It was also blatantly dishonest, but it was successful. Evolution sold like hot cakes, and it is still selling—so much so that anyone who questions it is thought to be biased by his religious convictions or not quite mentally respectable. It is interesting to note in this connexion that Etienne Gilson said during a course of lectures which he gave in America in 1971 that he had read Darwin's *Origin* three times but was still unable to understand it.*

During these American lectures, too, Gilson mentioned Herbert Spencer's claim that his own *Principles of Psychology,* which he published in 1855, contained in brief outline the doctrine of evolution and therefore anticipated the *Origin* (1859), which, Spencer complained, "is commonly supposed to have initiated it." Darwin, Gilson said, convinced people that Spencer was right. Then he made the dry comment: "It is an interesting example of historical humour." It is also, he might have added, an interesting example of disputed paternity, and one out of the usual run.

Another point made by Gilson was that Darwin referred repeatedly to the difficulty of distinguishing between species and varieties, and that in a letter written in 1853 he confessed that having studied barnacles for a whole year he was still not sure whether they constituted a separate species. All in all the French philosopher was somewhat hard on the only scientific theory of our time which, as someone says, has survived all attempts to substantiate it.

The Church's attitude to evolution is often described as obscurantist and unscientific, and those who say so usually add the rider "Look what it did to Galileo"—without, however, knowing what

Triumph Magazine, Washington, June 1971

it was exactly that it did to Galileo, for all the Church asked Galileo to do, and it makes the same request to the evolutionists, was not to put forward an unproven theory as fact. Catholics may —and many Catholics do—accept the (unproven) theory that the human body evolved from lower forms of matter, but they must believe that the human soul did not derive from anything already in existence, and that each human soul is directly created by God —which is something that science can neither prove nor disprove.

Pius XII, in his encyclical *Humani Generis*, emphasises the need for "the greatest caution and prudence" in discussing the theory of evolution (and though caution and prudence have their place in every scientific investigation, the evolutionists are not remarkable for either). Christians, he says, cannot lend their support to a theory which involves the existence, after Adam's time, of some earthly group of men who were not directly descended from Adam, or else supposes that Adam was the name given, not to the first man, but to some group of our primordial ancestors, because "it does not appear how such views can be reconciled with the doctrine of original sin as this is guaranteed to us by Scripture and tradition."

The Church, therefore, far from forbidding us to speculate, leaves us considerable latitude. But it is a latitude that I, for one, never feel tempted to avail myself of. If it is ever proved beyond all reasonable doubt (and so far the efforts in that direction have been anything but convincing) that our human bodies evolved from pre-existing forms, I shall bow my head, but in the meantime I refuse to believe that I am descended from a branch of the primates that has done rather well for itself.

I grant the many points of resemblance between myself and the chimpanzee, and there is no disputing the similarities in our anatomical frameworks, but then the skinned rabbit in the college laboratory where I tinkered with physiology was also frighteningly like me; and when I see a monkey peeling a banana, or swinging from branch to branch, or searching for fleas (and in two at least of these activities he could give me points) I do not rush to the conclusion that he is a poor relation whose ancestors failed to jump on the evolutionary wagon. What strikes me is, not that we are superficially alike, but that we are basically and fundamentally unlike. In the eyes of a monkey there is an emptiness, at once pitiful and revealing, that puts me back on my pedestal, and when I look at him I am face to face with something which in a billion light years could not produce a descendant capable of coping with the intellectual difficulties of addition with carrying.

4

Suddenly at

His Residence . . . .

I had a beginning, and I shall also have an end. Part of me—
not the part that thinks, and dreams, and plans, and grasps
spiritual form, but part of me nevertheless—will decay in time.
(Though even this, those who demand proofs for everything must
take on trust, since the only proof for it is the proof from analogy.)
My physical body, this conglomerate of bone, fat, muscle, and
conduits, will cease its vital functions sooner or later and crumble
into a horror that will generate gases and smells. Later there will
be nothing left but a scaffolding of bone, and later still the enduring bones will crumble into a nothingness of dust.

I am loved now, but when the end comes it will be the duty of
those who love me best to see that I am deposited where I will not
cause plague or pestilence. They will have my name cut on a brass
plate and a headstone, and they will know what these superscrip-
tions commemorate—which is certainly not the residue that is
referred to, with a certain nicety of idiom, as "the remains." This
they will bury deep and cede to the worms and the bacteria.

Few things are as swift and sudden as the transition from life
to death. Even a long-expected death that comes at the end of a
long illness is bafflingly sudden, and we can say of every man's
going that he went out like a light. When the breathing, living
body changes instantaneously into something utterly different—
and the change is always instantaneous—we say "He's gone," but

if the body were weighed immediately before and immediately after death the weights would tally. If there were a roll call of organs down to the tiniest physical components there would be none missing. Clearly something has gone, but it is not something that could be revealed in an autopsy: it is the life principle, the animating soul, indestructible and eternal.

Believing this we part company with those who let the problem go by default and are convinced that you and I, like all who have gone before us—philosophers and shepherds, ploughmen and plumbers—will vanish into nothingness in due course.

The prevalence of this chilling and comfortless conviction was shown by the contributions to a "Symposium on Death" published in the *Observer* in 1968, to which various experts contributed. (What qualifications one needs in order to be considered an expert on death were not specified. Moreover—possibly to exclude bias —there was no believing Christian on the panel. Some months earlier the same newspaper featured a symposium on "Are we the last married generation?" and most of the contributors, who included cinema stars, stage personalities, and dance band leaders, answered in the affirmative. In fairness, however, it must be pointed out that many of them had had considerable experience of marriage.)

The members of the illustrious death watch committee were all of one mind. None of them had the slightest vestige of belief in an after-life. One of them, a distinguished consultant surgeon, wrote: "Death is a simple thing. There is no after-life, so we've got to keep this one going as long as we can." (What he meant by describing death as a simple thing he did not reveal; and if we've got to keep this life going as long as we can it would have been interesting to have had his views on abortion and euthanasia.)

Another member of the panel, a successful actor, wrote: "The lights are going out, and there's nothing but darkness." A fine exit line, provided that one is not making a final exit; it might not be

30

so comforting then. And an even more successful man of the theatre spoke of the fear of something after death and of the undiscovered (but existing) bourn from which no traveller returns.

C. Day Lewis, the Poet Laureate, wrote: "I don't feel the need to be preserved in any form. I don't think my individuality is worth preserving." Most of the poets would be slow to agree; and Herbert, Donne, and Manley Hopkins—to name only a few—spent their lives proclaiming the very opposite. If Mr. Lewis had been looking for a seconder of his own craft he would have had to search far. There would be no point in asking that sturdy rebel Dylan Thomas, who wrote of a dying man: "I prayed in the crouching room, by his blind bed." Hardy or Shelley might be the best bets.

Lady Gaitskell took a different line. "While I don't believe in a life after death," she said, "I can understand just how comforting such a faith would be for me." Is there a touch of condescension here, a linking of belief in an after-life with belief in Santa Claus and the efficacy of the four-leaved shamrock? Belief in a life after death is not only a comforting thing but ultimately the only comforting thing. Without it there is nothing to hope for, nothing to laugh at, no stuff of dreams, no logical basis for self-respect. But it is also a shattering thing. It puts reality in the place of shadows.

Bertrand Russell might have been cited. He was the great expert on the after-life. He would have none of it. He ridiculed the very notion of it, and proclaimed his passionate thesis in language of epic stature.

"That Man is the product of causes that have no prevision of the ends they are achieving," wrote Russell, "that his origin, his growth, his hopes and fears, his loves and beliefs, are but the outcome of accidental collocations of atoms, that no intensity of thought or feeling can preserve an individual life beyond the grave . . . all these, if not quite beyond dispute, are yet so nearly certain

31

that no philosophy which rejects them can hope to stand."* (The bumptiousness of Russell's "if not quite beyond dispute" is characteristic, and the philosophy which denies all his premises had stood for a heck of a long time.)

All is not lost, however. We can still thumb our noses at the mindless causes whose product we are. "Condemned to lose today his dearest, tomorrow to pass himself through the gates of darkness, it remains for Man only to cherish, ere yet the blow falls, the lofty thoughts that enoble his little day . . . to preserve a mind free from the wanton tyranny that rules his outward life; proudly defiant of the irresistible forces that tolerate for a moment his knowledge and his condemnation, to sustain alone, a weary but unyielding Atlas, the world that his own ideals have fashioned despite the trampling march of unconscious power."†

But if man is no more than a chance collocation of atoms, what meaning is there in his defiance, and what reason is there for thinking that the wanton tyranny that shapes his outward life leaves him an inner sanctuary in which he is free to think lofty thoughts—since from Russell's premise it must shape his inner life also? For that matter, how can his thoughts be "lofty"—or even his own—if his hopes and fears, his loves and beliefs, are shaped and determined by irresistible forces which have no prevision of the ends they are achieving?

Every philosophy worthy of the name is a philosophy of death. If each of us is merely a fortuitous interlude in a continuous interplay of material components, every question that philosophy might ask goes by default. All that is left to us is stoic fortitude and the will to struggle hopelessly against the tyranny that shapes us, until it tires of its play and allows us to sink into the void from which we came.

*Free Man's Worship
†Mysticism and Logic

The materialists and the atheists are strangely inconsistent, for they honour the bodies of their dead. We, when we pay this honour, have logic as well as faith on our side, believing as we do that the lifeless body of child, spouse, or parent, was once and will be again the temple of the Holy Spirit, but the Russells have no such belief. What they honour is a "chance collocation of atoms," part of the universal economy of matter and destined for successive arbitrary groupings; yet they mourn just as deeply as the rest of us, and love no less.

And why have the Russians pumped chemicals into the body of Lenin and preserved it for the veneration of the faithful, since in their bleak creed the Lenin who preached and plotted and hated was obliterated as soon as the breath left him? Is the exposition a temporary concession to superstition, a peepshow for the comfort of a people whose heritage is onion steeples and ikons and church bells and who, although they have been freed by public ordinance from monkish teachings, are still living on the spiritual investments of their fathers?

Death is the moment of truth, not only one's own death but the deaths of those we know and love. It raises the big question, the question that has been answered all through the centuries by belief in a life beyond the grave. This belief may be vague or specific, a matter of shaky reason or firm faith, but at all times and in all places it has been a part of human thought. Materialism is the most recent of heresies, and those who subscribe to it must be troubled at times by ancestral voices.

Russell's summing-up is arrogantly dogmatic. That human life is not preserved beyond the grave, he says, "if not quite beyond dispute" is almost certain. But how can it be almost certain, when in the very nature of things it cannot be proven? And if it is almost beyond dispute, why is it still disputed? The truth is that survival after death, so far as the ordinary man is concerned (since the philosophic proofs for the immortality of the soul are beyond the ordinary man) cannot—as an isolated thesis—be either proved or disproved. You either believe in it as an article of faith or, like the members of the *Observer* panel, write it off as a superstition which Science has discredited and modern man outgrown.

But if you write it off, every vestige of religious belief goes with it: our individual lives have neither purpose nor significance, our hopes, loves, dreams, and strivings are merely by-products of our chemical make-up, and we are the playthings of blind, impersonal forces. On the other hand, if you accept it, you are committed to some very serious thinking. Indeed in a sense it is only then that your serious thinking begins.

5
The Man Above

Belief in a deity, or deities, runs like a pattern through the thought and culture of all peoples of whom we have any knowledge. This, of course, is far from being a proof that God exists. Indeed it is often advanced to prove the very opposite, and anyone who is not familiar with this sort of argument has obviously been missing his Sunday magazine supplements.

Primitive man, so the story runs, feeling himself small and defenceless in the presence of the forces of Nature, made attempts to placate them; he worshipped the moon and the stars, he made obeisance before thunder and lightning. But primitive man, of course, did nothing of the sort. He worshipped personal gods: the sun god, the moon god, the thunder god. Seeing power in the heavens, he postulated sources and origins for it.

It has even been suggested that primitive man based his belief in another world on the fact that when he dreamed at night he was no longer subject to the limitations of time and space. Waking in the morning, then, and finding himself back in his kraal, he concluded (being a primitive man) that he had visited a spirit world during the night. But there are no grounds for believing that a Samoan who lived in the first century would be any more likely to come up with this naive explanation of dreams than a New Yorker living in the twentieth—unless we assume that primitive men, of necessity, were primitive thinkers. But the quality of human thought, it will be pointed out, is always improving, and, in the past, magic and religion were closely intertwined. Our great-great-grandparents, for instance, believed in charms and spells and occult influences, whilst we, living in the scientific age, know that there is a rational explanation for everything (except, perhaps, the fact of our being here at all).

The boot, however, is on the other foot. Religion and magic do not go together. One thrives where the other decays. "Superstition," Chesterton points out, "recurs in all ages, especially in rationalistic ages"; and he recalls a luncheon at which he defended the religious tradition against a panel of distinguished agnostics, "each of whom, before the end of our conversation, had procured from his pocket, or exhibited on his watch-chain, some charm or talisman from which he admitted he was never separated."* It is significant that the weakening of religious belief in our own time has coincided with a growing interest in astrology, and that in these enlightened days many a so-called rationalist shows his hand by putting his trust in horoscopes. The devil too is back in business (ironically enough, at a time when he has been banished from the religious knowledge programmes of many a Catholic school), the Black Mass has been revived, and hard-hatted suburbanites who commute daily to insurance offices perform witch dances by the light of the moon.

There is no evidence to support the belief that our ancestors were more credulous and more gullible than we are, or that the quality of human thought improves cumulatively; we preen ourselves on such achievements as television and the harnessing of nuclear power, but each generation begins where the last leaves off, the wheel was a mighty invention in its day, and some of the best thinking of all time was done centuries before the internal combustion engine. By digging into the earth and sorting flint axes and

* The Everlasting Man

36

broken pottery we can get some idea of how our primitive ancestors lived, but it is dangerous to judge the quality of their thinking
by the quality of their artefacts. The brains which devised the
computer were not better than the brains which thought out the
abacus, and the fact that Edison and Einstein arrived late in the
play does not necessarily place them above Euclid or Archimedes.

Belief in a Supreme Being, too, was always linked, not just with
dependence and supplication, but also with worship (which was
His due) and a moral code (which expressed His will). The Great
Spirit was not remote and unregarding. He saw and approved, or
saw and disapproved. All this has been dismissed as no more than
the efforts of primitive men to ascribe a supernatural sanction to
their tribal mores, but an alternative explanation suggests itself at
once: if there is a God, surely it is reasonable to assume that our
relationship with Him was not left to men to puzzle out for
themselves, at various times and in different places, but that belief
in a Creator and in a God-given moral code was written into the
title deeds of human nature.

Moreover, if the universal belief in a Great Spirit was no more
than a crop of myths, why was it universal? Some exceptions,
surely, might have been expected, and there should have been
some primitive peoples who were content to eat and procreate and
sing songs and see the green earth as their only heritage. But
primitive men were never, it would seem, quite as primitive as that.
They sinned lustily, but—unlike the sinners of the modern permissive society—they did not believe that private judgment was the
sole arbiter of conduct.

But the label "primitive man" is a question-beggar, and it is
invariably used in a pejorative sense. It conjures up a shaggy,
dim-witted creature, lately come down from the trees and totally
unfitted for higher thought, and we have grown so used to this
concept that we fail to see how much of it is conjectural. Thus,
as Chesterton points out somewhere, it is commonly assumed that

primitive man got himself a mate by knocking her over the head with a stone axe and dragging her off to his cave—a gratuitous assumption which is echoed from school text to school text as if it were as certain as the date of Waterloo, and which would seem to indicate that until recent times human mating was based on a one-way attraction. Again it is taken for granted that primitive peoples lived in caves. This may well be true, but we have no proof —except the kind of proof that an archaelogist of the future, digging in the ruins of Paris, might adduce to support the thesis that the pictures in the Louvre were the work of folk who had married quarters there.

The concept of primitive men as slow-witted blunderers fits so neatly into the theory of evolution that it is practically a corollary of it. It is not so easily adjusted, however, to the traditional teaching that the human race is descended from a single pair of ancestors who, before they sinned and fell, were uniquely favoured in the matter of intellect and infused knowledge, and who knew from the first moment of their existence much that we have to learn by trial and error.

And if Adam was created with tremendous endowments of grace and intellect it it reasonable to assume that his knowledge of God did not die with him but was passed on to those who came after him. It is just as reasonable to assume that the story thinned down as the vast, earth-cumbering genealogical table arrowed out, and that its theological content lost its hard edges in places, but that the fundamentals remained and that some knowledge of and belief in a Creator to whom men owe worship and obedience seeped through to all races and peoples.

But belief in God is not simply part of our racial inheritance. It is a personal conviction that follows from the stirrings of conscience—that timeless monitor which has both a critical and a judicial office and which gives testimony that there is an objective moral law independent of our feelings and inclinations. Newman

38

develops this point at length, contrasting the feelings of fear, guilt, and confusion which certain acts often pleasurable in themselves arouse in us with the inward peace that follows other acts which are often painful in themselves, and makes the point that both involve the recognition of an intelligent Being as their exciting cause.

"We do not feel remorse before a horse or a dog," he says. "We have no remorse or compunction at breaking a human law. 'The wicked flees when no one pursueth.' Why then does he flee? Whence his terror? Who is he that he sees in solitude, in darkness, in the hidden chambers of his heart? If the cause of these emotions does not belong to this visible world, the Object to which his perception is directed must be supernatural and divine; and the phenomena of conscience, as a dictate, avail to impress the imagination with the picture of a Supreme Governor, a Judge, holy, just, powerful, all-seeing, retributive."*

Two objections are commonly advanced against the concept of a God-given objective moral law. The first is that if there were such a law its ordinances would be honoured everywhere and enshrined in the moral codes of all peoples; but moral codes differ, so the objective moral code is a myth. But differences in the moral codes of peoples, as Maritain points out, prove nothing against the objective moral law "any more than a mistake in addition proves anything against arithmetic, or the mistakes of primitive peoples for whom the stars were holes in the tent that covers the earth prove anything against astronomy."†

Again, the most striking thing about the moral codes of peoples past and present is, not that there are divergencies, but that they have so much in common. Murder and stealing, for instance, are prohibited in all codes, and even in the least developed communi-

*An Essay in Aid of a Grammar of Assent
† The Rights of Man and the Natural Law

ties the laws governing sexual morality are strikingly close to the Mosaic ordinance. It would seem then that we have to choose between a coincidence and a revelation: the coincidence being that at different times and in different places all the peoples of whom we have any knowledge evolved moral codes which in essentials approximate to a single moral code; the revelation, that God speaks to every heart, and that all men are equipped with a built-in censor which enables them to determine, in broad fields of conduct and with something approaching unanimity, the difference between right and wrong.

It is argued too that our ideas of right and wrong derive from experience and are related to the common good. Thus murder and theft are wrong, not because they are prohibited by the natural law, but because they are disruptive of public order and are offences against the community. But the sense of right and wrong is personal, not communal. The struggle of conscience which is involved when a man is tempted to steal from a wealthy corporation, or to murder an ailing wife so that he can marry his secretary, is one which concerns only himself and is not related to the good of the community.

It is significant too that those who reject the notion of the objective moral law maintain that certain actions are just and others unjust, and so plead before a court whose existence they deny, since if there were no set of generally accepted principles there would be no point in appealing to one's neighbour's sense of justice and fair play. The very fact that we ask those we argue with to "see" our point of view indicates that we assume in them the existence of a light which will enable them to see. Moreover, when we fail to convince, our feeling is not that the other fellow's code is different from ours but that we have bungled our case, and that had we put it properly he would have had no option but to agree.

In the past, framers of constitutions and legal codes invariably

40

began by citing certain inalienable human rights. The American Declaration of Independence (1776), for instance, states: "We hold these truths to be self-evident, that all men are created equal and that they are endowed by their Creator with certain unalienable rights." But much water has flown under the bridge in the meantime, and there can be little doubt that if this preamble were being drafted in these days there would be no mention of God Almighty. Certainly there is no mention of God in the United Nations Declaration of Human Rights, which lists freedom of conscience, liberty, religion, life, and security of person as inalienable human rights, but offers no source or justification for the existence of such rights—as if they had been granted to humanity for the first time by the General Assembly.

But all inalienable human rights are necessarily anterior to any human declaration of them—otherwise the qualification "inalienable" is meaningless—and their source and origin is the natural or objective moral law, which as St. Thomas says is our participation as rational beings in the Eternal Law.

The objective moral law is enshrined in our reason, with conscience holding a watching brief, reminding us of commitments, duties, sanctions. We are free to disobey, but we are not free of the law. If we disobey, we must take the consequences. The first consequence, as Newman says, is the realisation that we have offended. And one does not offend a law. One breaks a law; what one offends is a Person.

6
The Proofs

The average Christian, if he were asked to give a reasoned defence of his belief in God, would probably argue from the order and pattern that exists in the universe: the equipoise of the forces that determine the movements of the heavenly bodies and the swing of the schedule-keeping tides; the unvarying sequence from bud to leaf fall; the tiny seed that holds within itself the spread of a giant oak. Then, ruling out blind chance and "trial and error of matter," he would point to omniscience and omnipotence as the only answer.

He might also mention the fertilized ovum from which he sprang, that infinitesimal speck which, with incredible energy and glutton speed, acquired for itself within a few weeks the rudiments of organs and conduits; might speak of the complicated mechanism of his own adult body, which attends to elimination, growth, digestion, replacement, and a dozen other processes, juggles with amino acids, enzymes, and catalysts, and programmes the work of the 35 million glands in his stomach (give or take a few million) with the precision of a computer. Design being given, he might say, we must assume the existence of a designer, and so are forced to bring God into the picture.

Philosophically, they tell me, this argument has a lowly rating. But it is only the professional philosophers who say so, the folk whose theses in the learned quarterlies, buttressed by small-print citations, are so often a weariness of the flesh; for the ordinary Christian it has a ring of conviction.

And in this field the ordinary Christian is not at such a disadvantage as one might think, for the very scantiness of his loading keeps him from going off the rails. He simplifies perhaps, and he leans heavily on faith, but perhaps for that very reason his thinking is sound as far as it goes. When he speaks of "the Man Above," for instance, he is not thinking of a man like himself, or even of a superman; but he is certainly thinking of a Person, which is what really matters.

He is not thinking of a far-off, impersonal deity who runs everything by remote control, but of a loving God Who is as near to him as his elbow and as far away as the most distant star. The philosophers and theologians say the same thing in terms which, though more precise and rigorous, are necessarily fumbling and unsatisfying, since the finite mind can never prison in words the transcendent, absolute God Who is beyond and above all we can think about Him, Who is eternal, omniscient, omnipotent, all-pervading, the origin and end and explanation of all mutable contingent things.

The existence of God can be proved from reason, but the famous proofs of Aquinas, which are developments of the proofs advanced by Greek philosophers sixteen centuries earlier, are not for everyone; and even for those who can follow them they are convincing but not always coercive. Pascal, who was certainly capable of following them, said of them that they are grasped for the moment but forgotten an hour afterwards. For Pascal, the way to God is through Christ, Who claimed to be God, proved the truth of His claim by His miracles, and fulfilled the Old Testament prophecies to the letter; and all through the ages this has been the way of the countless millions who accepted the existence of the Man Above as they accepted the existence of the Polar Seas.

Scholarship and sophisticated arguments are not the complete

44

answer; for if there is a God to be known and loved (and any other kind is unthinkable) it would be contrary to justice (and He must be just) that certitude regarding His existence should be the monopoly of those who are equipped to study metaphysics; for if God is a reality to be known and loved, not a problem for the delectation of the dons, He must be as accessible to the ploughman as to the intellectual.

Moreover, as Etienne Gilson points out, very few people are qualified for metaphysical speculation—whence, he says, the dissatisfaction of many with the metaphysical proofs. The trouble is, perhaps, that when we study the proofs for God's existence we are looking for the kind of certitude we find in the mathematical proof of the formula that the difference of two squares is the product of the sum and difference of their roots; and the proofs for God's existence do not bring this kind of certitude, else all the professors would be theists. A house may be wired for electricity, but there can be no light until the current is turned on, and the light of faith is a gift of God.

One of the proofs for the existence of God is the argument from contingency. Everything in the universe is derivative, dependent on its constituent parts, the result of things or forces anterior to itself. The human embryo evolves from the male semen and the female ovum, the growing plant is provisioned by moisture, the molecule is a grouping of constituents. Nothing is self-explanatory. Everything is a result, a consequence, a chain of cause and effect. All things have a history and derive from other things which in their turn have a history.

But reason jibs at an infinite series of contingencies, and also at the notion that there was a time when nothing existed—since if at one time nothing existed it would have been impossible for anything to begin to exist. Thus we must either let the problem go by default, as too big for us, or conclude that there must always have been in existence something which exists of necessity and by

45

virtue of its nature; a Being who always was and always will be, and who is the source and origin of all else. This Being we call God.*

An argument like this, however, is not laced with fire. It inspires no passion of belief. Nor does it involve any commitment, other than an intellectual assent which, as Pascal says, may not last an hour. It will buttress faith, but it will not inspire it unless God speaks when the thinking is done.

Besides, the biggest questions still remain. Has this infinite God, whom we have sought out, sought us out? What are our duties towards Him? What does He ask of us? And if we are His people, how and when has He revealed himself to us? How can we know and love and serve the unknowable God unless He has spoken?

Which brings us back to the Israelites of old, who were oppressed and enslaved by Babylonians, Egyptians, Persians, and Romans, and who, compared with their neighbours, produced little of worth in art, science, or philosophy. But they did produce a literature, a unique literature which tells the story, not only of their wanderings and vicissitudes, but of their status as God's chosen people. God spoke to them and made a covenant with them. He gave them inspired leaders and prophets. He fed them with manna and quails in the wilderness, and let them pass dry-shod through the desert sea. They were God's children—His spoiled children. They rebelled and worshipped graven images, and they repented and were forgiven just as regularly. They broke the hearts of the prophets, but they clung to the vision and the promise. The Messiah would be born in Bethlehem of Judah, and He would set His people free.

*"It now appears that research under way offers the possibility of establishing the existence of an agency having the properties and characteristics ascribed to the religious concept of God."—Dr. Evan Harris Walker, theoretical physicist (Observer, 20 February, 1972). It would be interesting to know where, and by whom, this research is under way. The thesis, too, is self-contradictory, since the sought-for agency can be none other than God.

Even as a collection of stories or a historical record, the Old Testament is fascinating reading and a rich and colourful pageant, but the prophecies are what matter. If one man, Pascal says, had made predictions about the coming of the Messiah, it would have been significant; but for four thousand years a succession of prophets followed one another. Time is the test of any prophecy, and time vindicated the Old Testament prophecies, showing them for what they are—not just a forward-looking outlook on the part of the Jews, a fond hope that a saviour would arise and lead them to victory over their oppressors, not a delusion based on racial pride, but the record of God's converse with men, and His promises to them, during the long centuries between Adam's fall and the coming of His Son.

7
The Coming
of Christ

The concordance between the predictions of the Old Testament prophets and the story of Christ's life on earth as recorded in the New is something that cannot be explained except in terms of fulfillment. "The strongest proofs of Jesus Christ," says Pascal, "are the prophecies." Not the strongest, for the strongest were what Christ Himself said and did, but they fall into place like pieces of a jigsaw puzzle. And Christ had little patience with those who should have seen but failed to see their significance. "Too slow of wit, too dull of heart, to believe all the sayings of the prophets," He said to the two disciples on the road to Emmaus. Then, going back to Moses and the long line of the prophets, He interpreted the words used of Himself during the long centuries of waiting.

Christ came and lived among the people; preaching to them, curing the sick, banishing devils, raising the dead to life. He fed the multitude, and walked on the waters. He drew all men to Himself, and the crowds hung on His words.

He worked miracles, and He claimed to be God; not explicitly at first, for so stupendous a claim needed a conditioning even of His own. The Jews were used to prophets, and He, it seemed, was another prophet; the greatest of them, and one whose coming was foretold, but a man like themselves.

Yet, from the very beginning, He prepared them. When John,

in prison, sent two of his disciples to ask if He was the Messiah or if they were to wait for another, He answered: "Tell John what your own eyes and ears have witnessed; how the blind see, the lame walk, and lepers are made clean, how the dead are raised to life and the poor have the gospel preached to them."

He never quibbled, but when He said things like "None knows the Father except the Son, and none knows the Son truly except the Father," they thought He spoke in enigmas. But He spoke clearly and explicitly at last, saying, "Before Abraham was, I am," and the storm broke. The priests rent their garments, saying that He had blasphemed; and the people—the people whom He would have gathered as a hen gathers her chickens—dragged Him to Calvary and nailed Him up. Even there, the prophets followed; for not a bone of Him was broken, and the soldiers diced for His tunic.

His death seemed to disprove His audacious claim, for He had claimed to be God, and He had suffered mere men to crucify Him. Humanly speaking, He seemed a sorry imposter. But the real test was still to come. He had prophesied that He would rise again on the third day, and the Jewish scribes and elders (who knew the Old Testament backwards and should have known that this was the Promised One) placed a guard on the tomb lest His disciples should come and steal His body away and the new deceit be worse than the old.

He had claimed to be God, and it was a shattering claim; shattering and unique; for no one else, before or since—with the exception of the mentally deranged—has claimed to be God. As Chesterton says in *The Everlasting Man:*"Right in the middle of historic times there did walk into the world the original invisible being about whom the thinkers made theories and the mythologists handed down myths: the Man Who Made the World . . . It is simply false to say that other sages and heroes had claimed to be the mysterious master and maker of whom the world had dreamed and disputed. Not one of them had ever claimed to be anything of the sort. The most that any primitive myth had ever suggested was that the Creator was present at the Creation. But that the Creator was present . . . in the daily life of the Roman Empire—that is utterly unlike anything else in nature. It is the one great startling statement that man has made since he spoke his first articulate word . . . and it makes dust and nonsense of comparative religion."

How did Christ make good His claim? The old Penny Catechism answers very simply. "By dying on the Cross," it says, "Christ proved himself a real mortal man, and by raising himself from the dead He proved himself God."

His death on the Cross is an attested historical truth. What of His resurrection? The Jews placed a guard on His tomb, yet on Easter Sunday morning the tomb was empty; and the Jews, we may be sure, knowing what was at stake, had left nothing to chance. If ever there was a vigilant guard, it was here. Was the body spirited away? By whom? By the disciples, who had already panicked and dispersed? And in spite of the strong guard and the watchfulness of the scribes and elders? Given the fact of the empty tomb, there is only one explanation.

One of the most dramatic of all stories is the effect which Pentecost had on the disciples. They had hidden on Good Friday, their courage returned during the forty days, but after the Ascension it ebbed again. After Pentecost, however, they were men on fire. Their mission was to preach Christ crucified (not to expound the Gospels, which were still unwritten), and they went out (led by Peter, who had wept when the cock crew) to do the work of Him who had commissioned them. They went out exultantly, knowing that they would be delivered up to kings and princes. Suffering and martyrdom was to be their certain fate, yet their heads were high and they were humble and bold at once; humble, knowing their own weakness; bold, by virtue of the power that had been given them and the presence of the Holy Spirit who would teach them all things and abide with them forever. They knew their authority and their power; and the preface to their first incredible pronouncement was "It has seemed good to the Holy Spirit and to us."

Unlettered men, they became overnight a peripatetic school of theology, and in the beginning all who listened to them heard each in his own language. They were Jews to a man, nurtured in the Mosaic tradition, but now their mission was to Jew and gentile, circumcised and uncircumcised. This was their charge, and how were they equipped for it in view of their background and education? They seemed bound to fail, yet the fire in their hearts kindled a response everywhere, and the growth of the early Church was in itself a proof that this was God's work.

"What is really hard to believe," writes Augustine, "is the way the world came to believe. The fishermen whom Christ sent out were men unversed in the liberal arts, with no skill in language, armed with no rhetorical power. Yet they landed fish of every sort, not excluding those rare specimens, the philosophers. Three incredibilities are involved. It is incredible that Christ should have risen; it is incredible that the world should have believed a thing so unbelievable; it is incredible that men so unaccomplished, so rude and lowly, should have convinced men of something so incredible and convinced them so conclusively. The sceptics, of course, will shy at the first incredibility; but the second they must believe; and if they reject the third they have no explanation of a manifest fact."*

One thing must be remembered about the teaching of the apostles, and it is this: that it must have had a *content.* To state that they preached Christ and Him crucified is merely to state the basis on which all their teaching depended. In the early days, no

*The City of God, Book XII

doubt, mass conversions were frequent, the charisma of the apostles operated on many who heard them, and the Holy Spirit spoke directly to human hearts; but from the very beginning there must have been arguments, disputations, objections, and a corpus of theological knowledge to be stated and defended. What the apostles were doing was establishing a Church based on infallible truth, and the truth had to be propounded and safeguarded. Of necessity they worked as men might when sowing seed, but in the nature of things they could not be content with a single scattering. From the beginning, the Church was a structured community, hierarchically organized, and subject to the authority of the apostles and their successors in matters of faith as well as jurisdiction. This is stated explicitly by biblical scholars like Léon-Dufour, but it needs no endorsing by the experts, since it is clear, not only from the Acts and the letters of St. Paul, but also from the very terms of the problem. The apostles were founding a Church that was to last to the end of time, and there must have been title deeds, and a constitution, and accredited, authoritative custodians who would see to it that heresies would be nipped in the bud.

But not—and this is important—a written constitution, for the Gospels were not written until later.* There were records and transcripts in places, but the teaching of the apostles and the faith founded on it consisted mainly of oral tradition; of things heard and remembered, things preserved and passed on. Thus even as

---

*"Modern critics," writes Father John L. McKenzie, S. J., in his *Dictionary of the Bible*, "are generally agreed that St. Mark's Gospel was written in the decade 60–70; efforts to show an earlier or a later date have not been successful." Fragments of the Gospel of St. Mark found in Cave VII at Qumran, however, one of the smaller caves in the area where the Dead Sea Scrolls were discovered, and in a type of handwriting used during the period 50 B.C. to 50 A.D., give grounds for thinking that Mark was written during the lifetime of St. Peter, and this, if it is true, would throw a lot of biblical scholarship out of kilter. It would be particularly embarrassing to those critics who maintain that much of the theology of St. Mark's Gospel (the divine sonship of Jesus, the value of the crucifixion as atonement, etc.) is due to the interpolations of "second generation Christians" and represents a departure from the teachings of the "primitive Church."

53

late as the fourth century we find St. Basil writing: "Of the dogmas and preachings preserved in the Church, some we have from written teaching, others we have received in a secret way passed on to us from the tradition of the apostles."* It is nonsense to suggest that the apostles and the disciples (and there were seventy-two disciples) did nothing but call people to repentance and teach that Christ was the Son of God, and that dogma as we know it was a later accretion. What they were entrusted with and passed on was nothing less than the deposit of faith.

*On the Holy Ghost

8

The Primacy
of Peter

The pre-eminence of Peter is implicit in the New Testament; and the Evangelists, when they are listing the apostles, always put his name first. It was Peter who first preached to the people on Pentecost; it was Peter who presided at the selection of Matthias and at the Council of Jerusalem. Obviously he had power and authority, and three questions follow. Who gave him this power and authority? What was the nature of it? And did it die with him, or was it passed on to his successors?

There has been much juggling with the texts that supply the answers, but they speak for themselves. "Blessed art thou, Simon Bar Jona," said Christ after Peter's profession of faith at Caesar Philippi, "for flesh and blood has not revealed this to you, but my Father who is in Heaven. And I say to thee, thou art Peter, and upon this rock I will build my Church, and the gates of Hell shall not prevail against it. I will give to thee the keys of the kingdom of Heaven. Whatsoever thou shalt bind upon earth shall be bound also in Heaven, and whatsoever thou shalt loose upon earth shall be loosed also in Heaven."*

Christ was not promising Peter that his rulings would be honoured in Heaven and countersigned automatically. What He was saying was that Peter's decisions on faith and morals would be

*Matthew, 16: 15–20

55

infallibly true, and no other interpretation of the loosing and binding text holds water. The promise to Peter was not a blank cheque on which he could fill in the details as he thought fit. It was a guarantee of the guidance of the Holy Spirit.

Christ was the Way, the Truth, and the Life, and He was appointing someone to speak in His name. He was handing him over the keys, and endowing him with the authority and immunity from error that went with them.

First nomination, then installation, for after the Resurrection, having first asked, "Simon, son of John, lovest thou me more than these?" (not just "lovest thou me?" but "more than these") Christ said, "Feed my lambs, feed my sheep."* This was the language of metaphor, the language of the parables, but it needs no gloss. And again: "Simon, Simon, behold Satan has desired to have you that he may sift you as wheat. But I have prayed that thy faith may not fail, and do thou, once thou has turned again, strengthen thy brethren."† If words have any meaning, this is a definite commissioning which rules out any *primus inter pares* quibbling.

Hans Küng, hell-bent on watering down the power and authority of Peter and his successors, writes in *The Church:* "It is an absurd situation that the Petrine ministry which was intended, as Catholics in particular see it, to be a rock-like and pastoral ministry, preserving and strengthening the unity of the Church, should have become a gigantic, apparently immovable, insuperable and impassable block of stone barring the way to mutual understanding between the Christian Churches." The Petrine *ministry,* he goes on (and the italics are his) "appeared to men to be more and more a Petrine *dominion."* The phrase "more and more" should be noted. It suggests without explicit assertion (which is the Küng method) that the primacy of Peter and his successors has been

*John, 21: 17,18
†Luke, 22: 28–33

56

cumulatively exploited by the triumphalism of the Church ("triumphalism," that blessed neologism): and he wonders "if there is a way back, which would also be a way forward, from the primacy of dominion to the old primacy of service and ministry."

But the primacy was always both; was always a primacy of service and ministry on the one hand, and of dominion on the other. The popes have always been servants of their flocks (and the first twenty-three of them, including Peter, were martyrs), but when questions of faith or morals were to be decided they spoke with authority and exercised the dominion that had been given them. ("Feed my lambs, feed my sheep"—"strengthen thy brethren.")

"It is little short of scandalising," Küng goes on, "that each of the three texts used to prove the precedence of Peter is accompanied by passages which balance, if not obscure, the bright tones of the Petrine text. The three great promises are balanced by three serious failures . . . And if the promises in large letters on a gold background surround the Church of St. Peter like a frieze, it would be only right, to avoid misunderstandings, to add to them the three contrary incidents on a black background."

In all Küng's writings one misses the precision and clarity that are the marks of the mature theologian (but then he became a world-known theologian at thirty-three—an age at which the real masters were still serving their apprenticeship), and this outburst reads like an excerpt from an undergraduate debate. Peter had weaknesses and human failings, but no one knew this better than the Christ who commissioned him; and He commissioned him nevertheless. "Believe me, this night, before the cock crows, thou wilt thrice disown me," He said to Peter on the very night when He commanded him, "And do thou, once thou has turned again, strengthen thy brethren." Peter would fail, but he would turn again ("I have prayed that thy faith may not fail"), and after that there would be no more failures. The texts on the golden back-

57

ground need no balancing doubts, and the "contrary incidents," as Küng calls them, complete rather than take from their glory and significance.

Peter's primacy, and the infallibility that went with it (and infallibility was possessed by the other apostles too, but when and only when they acted in concert and with Peter as their head), have been bones of contention since the sixteenth century. But it is well to know what was attacked, and what is still being attacked: which is not so much the powers and prerogatives of Peter and his brethren as the apostolic succession. But if it all ended with the death of Peter, then the words of the risen Christ recorded in the last verses of St. Matthew are meaningless: "You, therefore, must go out, making disciples of all nations . . . and behold I am with you all days even to the end of the world." Christ did not preach only to His contemporaries, or die for one generation; and the Church that He founded—we have His own word for it—is to last to the end of time. If the apostles whom He commissioned had not the power to appoint accredited successors, then the whole thing was badly bungled and there can be no continuity of doctrine. And the first recorded action of the apostles after the Ascension, it is well to remember, was to co-opt and consecrate a successor to Judas. The eleven had been appointed by Christ Himself, but Matthias was selected by men, and he ranked with the rest and had the same credentials. The Church's constant teaching (and if it taught the opposite it would cut its own lifeline) is that the privileges, powers, and guarantees given to the apostles and to Peter as their head did not end with them but were passed on through the centuries by the laying-on of hands.

Hans Küng, in *The Church*, wriggles out of this basic truth, and after torrents of words and tiresome small-print qualifications, arrives at the conclusion: "The whole Church, and hence every individual member of it, stands in the line of succession to the apostles"; and he repeats himself at even greater length in his book

58

Infallibility, showing what one critic described as "a paralysing incapacity for coherence."*

Küng makes the following points:

(1) "As the immediate, primary witnesses and primary messengers of Christ, the apostles could not *a priori* be replaced or represented by any successors."

(2) "Even though there can be no new apostles, the mandate and function of the apostles remain . . . Apostolic mission and apostolic ministry, however, are carried on by the *whole* Church. *Every* Christian is in succession to the apostles."

The first of these luminous statements would seem to mean that dead men are dead and that the present-day bishops of the Catholic Church never walked with Christ in Galilee; and anyone who held the opposite would be certifiable. The second suggests its own rebuttal. If the mandate and the function of the apostles remain, surely the only place where they are to be found is in the dynastic line.

The old Penny Cathechism had a simpler approach. "The successors to the apostles," it said, "are the bishops of the Holy Catholic Church." Belief in the reality of the apostolic succession is firmly embedded in the tradition of the Church, and the whole case for the authenticity of her teaching depends on it. Unless the mandate was handed on through election and the action of the Holy Spirit, unless Christ's promises were for all time (that is, unless He meant what He said), continuity, credibility, and authority go by the board.

On this issue, the Church speaks and has always spoken with a single voice. Thus we find Ireneus of Lyons, one of the Fathers of the primitive Church, writing: "We can name the men who were appointed bishops by the apostles and their successors down to our own times," and asserting that these bishops never taught and

*W.H.Marshner: *Triumph* Magazine, June 1971

could not teach heresy since they inherited more than an office. St. Cyprian of Carthage, too, writing in the middle of the third century, cites the "On this rock" text, saying that anyone who does not assent to this source and principle of unity deserts the Chair of Peter; and in 432, when the Fathers had run into difficulties at the Council of Chalcedon and a legate brought Pope Leo's decision to them, their response was: "Peter has spoken through Leo."

Vatican I stated categorically that there could be no quibbling on this issue. "Whoever asserts," it declared, "that Peter's successors do not have the chief place in the whole Church, appointed by Christ the Lord, that is by divine right . . . let him be anathema." Vatican II, as a pastoral Council, was gentler in its language but equally sure of its ground (as Küng should know, since he was one of the experts who advised it): "That divine mission entrusted by Christ to the apostles will last to the end of the world, since the gospel which was to be handed down by them is for all time the source of all life for the Church. For this reason the apostles took care to appoint successors in this hierarchically structured society."

The clear and unequivocal statement of Vatican II is quoted by Küng in *The Church* with the comment: "There are no quotations from Scripture in support of this, simply the declaration." Later, characteristically, he seems to dither a little, and says: "The ministerial primacy of a single person is not contrary to Scripture. Whatever may be the justification for it, there is nothing in Scripture which would exclude such a ministerial primacy."

The appeal to Scripture as the final arbiter runs through all Küng's writings, and in urging a false ecumenism he constantly asserts this doctrine, which in its time has been largely responsible for the sundering of Christendom. It is even more disturbing and a still greater scandal to find the same view being urged by Cardinal Suenens, himself a successor of the apostles, who has said: "We must look first, not to any code of canon law, however venerable, but to the Gospels and the Acts of the Apostles, which immerse us directly in the mystery of Pentecost."*

John Eppstein minces no words in his comment: "This appeal to private judgement without regard to the tradition of the Church," he says, "is pure Protestantism and can be respected as such. But it is completely at variance with the whole spirit of the Roman Catholic Church as it has developed, and as, *pace* Cardinal Suenens, it was reaffirmed, though in new terms, by the Ecumenical Council."†

Citing the Gospels against the tradition and teachings of the Church which is their guarantor and accredited interpreter is mad theology. Moreover, apart altogether from the question of interpretation (and the Church is the infallible interpreter) the Gospels are not a complete record of what Christ taught, nor the Acts a synopsis of what the apostles taught. And it is not the New Testament which immerses us in the mystery of Pentecost. The charisma which inspired the Pentecostal Church has come down to all of us, not as a Gnostic inspiration linked with private interpretation of the Scriptures but through accredited teachers and valid sacraments, through the laying on of hands, and the apostolic succession, and the waters of baptism. It is the Church that guarantees the truth of the Gospels, and we should still be immersed in the mystery of Pentecost had they never been written.

*In an interview given to the editor of *Informations Catholiques Internationales* in May 1969.
†*Has the Catholic Church Gone Mad?*

9
Kneeling Before
the World

Maritain, in *The Peasant of the Garonne*, says that the con-
tempt for all created things which was professed by many of the
saints in the past led to a veiled Manicheism in Christian thought,
so that some spiritual writers came near to teaching—or at least
were understood as teaching—that all creation is evil and that
since the Fall there is nothing but corruption in the world. The
only thing to do, therefore, is to remain aloof from the world, lead
one's inner life, and seek salvation in flight. This false notion,
Maritain goes on, was set right by Vatican II, which put the
relation between the eternal and the temporal in proper perspective and reaffirmed the natural goodness of all created things.

Whether this Manicheism, veiled or otherwise, was ever as
operative as Maritain thinks is open to doubt. But there is no
doubting what he says next. The wheel has turned full circle, he
observes; the new error is worse than the old, and many Catholics,
misunderstanding (or misrepresenting) what Pope John had in
mind when he spoke of *aggiornamento*,* say that the principal task
of the post-Conciliar Church is to adapt itself to the world and
accept its norms. "In large sectors of the world," Maritain goes on,

*Christopher Derrick, in *Trimming the Ark*, feels entitled "to cast gentle, charitable
doubts upon the human prudence of Pope John," and to suggest that "in launching the
highly rhetorical term *aggiornamento* upon a Church somewhat pent-up and even
hysterical, he did a great deal of harm."

"and it is the clergy who set the example, hardly is the word 'world' mentioned than a gleam of ecstasy lights up the faces of one and all."

(Teilhard's face, of course, lit up as far back as 1934, when he wrote: "If by consequence of some internal upheaval I came to lose successively my faith in Christ, my faith in a personal God, my faith in the spirit, it seems to me that I should continue to believe in the World. The World—the value, the infallibility, and the goodness of the World—such in the final analysis is the only thing in which I believe."*)

Maritain calls this phenomenon "kneeling before the world— the pure world of science, the world of astronomers, geologists, biologists, psychologists, ethnologists, technicians, and states- men." And "kneeling" is the right word, since what is involved is prostration and surrender: trimming the Church's teaching to fit in with contemporary notions of sexual morality; blurring the distinction between the Church teaching and the Church taught; seeing authority as coming from below (from the "people of God") and not from above; seeing the ministerial priesthood as differing in degree only (not in kind) from the priesthood of the laity (collar-and-tie priests, "call me Leslie" priests, and the dangerous half-truth that the consecrating minister "presides" over the weekly gathering of the people of God); and the wild heresy that priests, nuns, and religious are doing God's work best when they head protest marches, join in sit-ins and lie-downs, or even take to the hills and fight with the revolutionaries. The Church must be desacralized (break the statues, hide the tabernacle, stop messing about with holy water) and democratised (let the people choose their rulers). It dare not stand aside whilst the world moves on (though the only alternative is to jump on the bandwagon now and be jettisoned later as a defused anomaly).

*Comment je Crois

64

The priests who rebel against ecclesiastical authority are all too easily seduced by the rebels against political authority, and as Malcolm Muggeridge once said, there is no movement so disruptive that a gathering of dog-collars cannot be found to spearhead it. And the starry-eyed priests and nuns who take part in "peace marches" and "freedom demonstrations" are prone to selective indignation. They protest against South African footballers but not against Russian runners, they thunder against the "imperialistic war-mongers" but not against the Viet Cong. Their support and their sympathy go always to the forces of the Left. Capitalism is the enemy, and it must be overthrown by revolutionary action. The Church was always on the side of money and power, and if it is to rehabilitate itself it must take its place at the barricades. Pope John is invoked as the patron of the new Crusade—and blatantly misquoted in the process. For Pope John, far from giving the green light to socialism, echoed his predecessors and said that whenever pride of place is not given to private enterprise two things follow: political tyranny and a shortage of consumer goods.*

The rebel priests cherish the fond hope that their services will be remembered and requited when the revolution comes to pass. But history proves the opposite. The learned clerks and the intellectuals are useful when the revolution is beginning; they give it a facade of intellectual respectability and reassure the common people; but when the Bastille is captured theirs are the first heads to fall.

The notion that the Church's primary concern is the attainment of social justice and political freedom leads inevitably to disaster, for it is founded on a lie; and the lie is that the City of God can be established by ordinance and revolutionary action. The real work of the Church is to preach the gospel and administer the sacraments. Its mission is to the heart of man, its concern is

Mater et Magistra

65

with his soul. It lays down the principles of social justice, but it is not its business to implement them.

The admonition "Seek ye first the kingdom of Heaven" establishes a priority which many latter-day Catholics seek to reverse. Their doctrine is "Seek ye first better living conditions, social justice, and political freedom by revolutionary action, and the grace of God will come in due course." But things don't work out that way. Only Christlike men can establish a just social order, since men must reform themselves before they reform society, and if religion is put on the long finger it is sure to languish.

Without prayer and worship and belief, social work, however altruistic its motives, can easily become a new kind of materialism, and a proper spiritual outlook is the one thing that prevents service to one's fellows from blurring one's sense of values. Blessed is he who hungers and thirsts after justice, and serving the community is a noble vocation, but the community has no meaning apart from the individuals who comprise it; men must be good before they are wise, and the only real foundation for social justice is obedience to the natural law and the commandments.

This is why Communism, in all the countries where it has been imposed, has failed dismally to make men free, happy, or prosperous. Based on naturalism and atheism, it sees man, not as an autonomous entity with God-given rights, but as a faceless cell in the community, to which he is indebted for such rights as are conceded to him. After this fundamental misconception the rest follows, for the natural law, clarified by revelation, lays down the precepts by which man must be guided if he is to be true to his nature and his actions consistent with right reason.

It is strange to find so many Catholics seeing capitalism as the source of all our economic ills and Communism as the only hope for the future, although capitalism has changed radically from the early days of the Industrial Revolution, and although—because of the growing strength of trade unionism and increasing govern-

66

ment control—it has been shorn of its one-time despotic powers. Moreover, in all capitalist countries, and in all countries with a mixed economy, the last half-century has seen a cumulative improvement in social conditions and a levelling-up of classes. This is freely conceded by no less a person than Milovan Djilas, who was once next in line of succession to Tito. "Technological development and free forms of ownership in the West," he writes, "have reached a point where the top layer of the working class, if not indeed its main bulk, has been merging with the middle class, the bourgeoisie." And again: "If western Capitalism has not disappeared, it no more resembles its adolescent image than contemporary East European Communism resembles the blessed classless society of Marx's dream." Considering its source, this is a testimony which cannot be easily discredited.

"Communism," Djilas says, "suffers from all the ills which it had justly stigmatised as the sins of Capitalism"—a striking admission from one who spent three years in a Yugoslav prison for his Communist beliefs. And although he is an atheist, his explanation of the Communists' failure comes very near the Catholic position, for he speaks of "the inevitability of violence and corruption in human beings—in the mass and as individuals—once Marxism in its totality is applied to society, or, more strictly speaking, is imposed on society."*

The Catholic intellectuals who think that Marxism can be baptized and fumigated should bone up on its classic texts. Wittingly or unwittingly they have come to terms with the materialistic ethic, which is that once mankind has freed itself from the religious myths that have alienated it from its true destiny—the control of the material environment—it will move on inexorably to the New Jerusalem of peace, justice, brotherhood, and prosperity. Religion, to the Marxist, is a canker that must be rooted out.

*The Unperfect Society

Its sights being set on another world, it deludes the people with promises of "pie in the sky" and so conditions them that they either acquiesce in their own exploitation or endure it meekly in the belief that we have not here a lasting city.

No one, as yet, has suggested that we *have* a lasting city, but our individual leases will probably be stretched in time to a hundred years or more. So the spectre of overpopulation is being raised, and many articulate Catholics have been frightened into recommending—or at least not opposing—such panic measures as contraceptives for teenagers, abortion on demand, and compulsory family limitation. But the anti-pollutionists do not stop at that. They want not only fewer people but nicer people, and they suggest that undesirables should be compulsorily sterilized, lest they breed equally undesirable offspring who might become a tax burden. The pressure should be eased at the other end too, and the incurable or the senile should be snuffed out mercifully before they become dotty, incontinent, and a charge on society.

Kneeling before the world is a double idolatry, for it commits us of necessity to kneeling before ourselves. The last fifty years have seen incredible advances in human knowledge: knowledge of our own bodies, of plant life and nutrition, of physics, chemistry, weather forecasting, drugs, and outer space. But we have let our achievements go to our heads. All we have done—all we can ever hope to do—is to discover laws and principles and experiment with existing substances, putting this and that together and finding that the result solves a problem or answers a need. We boast about our "discoveries," but we can only discover what is already there, and we forget that someone must have put it there. The most our scientists can do is to potter about in God's workshop, and both the tools and the data are provided for them.

No sooner had we landed men on the moon than we began to talk about "the conquest of outer space," though the moon is a mere 240,000 miles away from us, and some constellations have been receding from the earth since time began at the not inconsiderable speed of 186,000 miles *a second*. The truth is that the earth and the moon, as stellar distances go, are as near as almost touching beads on a child's abacus, and, far from having conquered outer space, we have not yet begun to nibble at it. Moreover, if the speed of our spaceships should increase tenfold during the next decade our furthest voyages would bring us no more than a flea's hop from the Pole-flattened planet on which we live.

Peering upwards with radio telescopes or radar feelers we find one kind of infinity, and our physicists, winkling out the secrets of atoms and neutrons, see another and peel skins from an inexhaustible onion. The empyrean is mirrored in every cell.

The most we can do is look under stones and come upon wonders. Aristotle and the Greeks did the same long centuries ago, but they used their minds in default of lasar beams and speculated on the real problem—the problem of who put the wonders there for us to find.

If we postulate an omnipotent God as the source of all the patterns and laws we observe in the universe, we are spared a lot of profitless thinking. The humanist will sneer at this as a non-solution that an illiterate washerwoman might accept but is beneath the notice of anyone who is not prepared to take things on trust. But it is well to remember two things: first, that this answer has been accepted by philosophers all through the ages; and second, that it is more intellectually satisfying than the alternative one, which is that unthinking matter devised laws for its own better functioning and transmitted such ordinances as that every acorn should grow into an oak, that bees should make honey, and that water should always and everywhere seek its own level—an explanation so naive that although it has been accepted by many of the professors it would be rejected out of hand by all the washerwomen.

The Christian explanation is blindingly logical, and it leaves no

69

loose ends. Granted the nature of God, everything falls into place. If He alone is necessarily existent, if He is omniscient, omnipotent, and omnipresent (and if He exists at all He must be all of these), He is the source and origin of all things else and the choreographer of every dance of electrons. Nor is He just an absentee landlord managing His affairs by remote control, or a master craftsman who, having wound up all creation, leaves every part of it to tick on blindly and fend for itself. The universe is a vast and bewildering place, but every part of it is under His personal supervision, and no dog barks without His help.

Kneeling before the world is the ultimate blasphemy. It replaces worship of the Creator by worship of the thing made, and it ends in the apotheosis of man himself. It looks towards the coming of the Nietzschean *Ubermensch*, who will lord it over lesser men, stride the earth like a god, and control it as his own personal bailiwick.

Teilhard muddled his terms when he said that if he lost his faith in Christ, in a personal God, and in the spirit, he would still believe in the world, for all that would be left to him then would be belief in himself. And the same choice is before all of us: either we must hold to our faith in Christ and in a personal God, or we must kneel before the world and see our own image reflected in it.

10
Free Will

Sir, we know our will is free, and there's an end on't.
—Samuel Johnson

The Church's teaching on free will—which seems to but does not clash with the concept of an all-knowing God—is that normally each of us has the power to choose this and reject that; that we are autonomous, self-governing entities, and, as such, answerable for all our actions. Admittedly, when we are between waking and sleeping, heavily drugged, or have been subjected to the brutal "conditioning" which has become a feature of life in certain parts of the world, the power of free will may become weakened or inoperative for a time, but this is no more an argument against free will than dirty spectacle lenses are an argument against eyesight.

The exercise of free will, like everything else, is subject to God's will, since we can do nothing, not even sin, without His consent; but His consent is never withheld. He never forces our wills; and He never allows any created intelligence, devil or angel, to force them. The angels, both good and bad, can suggest, encourage, and incite, but they cannot compel. Nor can they foretell, in any given circumstance, how we shall act. They may guess—and, knowing us as they do, and having angelic intelligence, their guesses are at times odds-on bets—but the final choice is ours. Only God knows what we shall do (not what we must do); all the rest must wait and see.

71

The will is God's outright gift to us; and yet, having given it, He asks it back, and His death is the price He offers. There is a seeming anomaly here, but only until we remember *how* He asks it back; for He asks it, not as a once-for-all ceding but under a continuously renewable lease. He becomes the tenant of the property from instant to instant—if we listen to His pleading—but it remains always *our* property, and we can dispose of it as we please. He wants us to obey Him always whilst still retaining the power to disobey. He has made us free and autonomous, and He wants the service and obedience of the free and autonomous. Nothing less will satisfy Him. He has drawn up the contract so that He, who made us, is the eternal suitor, and we, who are dependent on Him for everything, are forever free to grant or withhold.

There is mystery here. The surrendering of the gift of our free will, the ceaseless instant-to-instant ceding of it for which He pleads, is the perfecting of the will; for the good of the will is to act in conformity with the will of God. Our self-ness grows and ripens when we seem to surrender it, and what seems like blind and slavish subservience is really self-assertion and self-expression. Each one of us is made to a master plan of God's making, and the more we conform to that plan the more *real* we become. For we are men, not maggots. Every maggot is simply another term in an endless progression of maggots, and when you have seen one maggot you have seen them all; but each human being is a new creation, unlike anything else that ever was or ever will be, and created to play a part in God's plan for the world. But God does not shape us, except with our consent and in so far as we cooperate with His will. The choice is ours, for better or worse. We can become more and more like what He wants us to be, which means tending more and more towards our own perfection, or we can substitute our own wills for His, moving away from the splendour He has planned for us and back towards the nothingness from which we came. We do not write the play; we merely act in it; and

72

it is left to each of us to decide when and how far he will follow the script.

The only ones who give star performances are the saints. The rest of us often feel that we have been given roles which do not suit us, or demand too much of us, or bring us nothing but frustration and defeat. Christ foresaw all this, for He warned us that we must take up our cross daily and follow Him, which in stage language means that we must have the utmost confidence in the Producer. We may have doubts and black moments, but we can be sure of one thing: that God does not botch His casting, and that if we follow the script He will groom each one of us for stardom.

This is the strangest of plays, for there are no extras, and each actor plays the lead. Each of us is born at a certain time and in a certain place because there is something that needs doing, something which, because of our gifts and endowments (not to speak of our failings and shortcomings) no one else could do as well, and every mother's son of us is called and commissioned as surely as were Paul and Xavier.

In the fierce religious controversies which accompanied the Reformation, free will, as the power of choice which brings us to hell or heaven in the end, was one of the bones of contention. Granted, its opponents urged, that there is a God who knows from all eternity who of us will be saved and who damned, our wills cannot be the deciding factor. If we are born with destination tags already affixed we will be saved or damned in spite of ourselves; if the examination results are known before the papers are set, the candidate's showing is neither here nor there and the ploughing has been done beforehand.

God's foreknowledge of what is going to happen, however, is no more than a figure of speech, for there is no before or after in God's knowledge. There is no progression in God, no sequence, no history, no looking ahead. God is outside time. He sees and knows in the eternal present.

But if God *knows* that I will be saved, it can be argued, then I am home and dried, and my salvation is assured; and if He *knows* that I will be damned, then there is nothing that I can do about it. The answer is that God's knowledge does not *determine* my actions. It leaves me free. The philosophical difficulty is there admittedly, but it hinges on God's being outside time. His knowledge of what is going to happen no more determines the outcome than my knowledge of the result of a football match that was played yesterday has any bearing on the play when I see the game on a television screen this evening.

God's eternal present is a concept at which my finite reason jibs, but my reason jibs too at the time sequence in which I live, move, and have my being—this endless fusion in which yesterday becomes today and today becomes tomorrow, and which boils down to an eternal present. My past is gone forever, and my future (which is not guaranteed even while I type this page) has still to come. Our "present" slips away from us, hour by hour and instant by instant, and this is an impoverishment of our being—a limitation, a rationing. God, however, knows no such rationing. His Being does not come to Him in installments, and to see His omniscience as an argument in favour of predestination and against the reality of our free will is to apply to Him the conditions of our own being.

It is difficult to think of God as being outside time, but to think of being inside time, as we are, is not plain sailing either. Where, for instance, is the past that was yesterday? And where is tomorrow lurking? Has time past or time still to come any reality? Even the infinitesimal speck of time that we call the present is a will-o'-the-wisp. It is gone before we can grasp it (but gone where?), and it is "now," and not "tomorrow," that never comes.

Time is as much a mystery as eternity. All we can say about it is that it passes. It is the measure of things that change, and we, like all created things, are subject to it. We change physically not

74

only from day to day but from hour to hour: renewing our cells, burgeoning or shrinking, ageing inexorably. But we are changing also in a much more important way: we are constantly moving towards God or away from Him, and it is our own wills—not His —that set the course. This is our privilege. It is also God's gamble: a gamble which seems a negation of His wisdom, but is really the ultimate measure of His love. He has made us in His image and likeness, but He pays us the awful compliment of leaving us free to follow or hang back. His mercy, like all His attributes, is infinite, but humanly speaking it has one limitation, for there is one thing He will not do—He will not save us in spite of ourselves.

We are constantly changing, forever becoming holier or less holy, and the result at any moment of time depends on our own wills. But there is an end result. The account is not kept open forever. A final balance will be struck sooner or later, and it will stand for all eternity. As long as the breath is in us, our wills are free, but at the moment of death they are fixed forever.

Hell or heaven, reward or punishment—how can we equate this dread picture of the end of it all with the concept of a loving and merciful God who desires nothing but our happiness? The answer is that we *must* equate it, in view of the repeated warnings of this same loving and merciful God when He walked the earth. Moreover, it is not He who condemns. He passes sentence admittedly, but we condemn ourselves and are our own prosecutors.

Moreover, the hearing will be loaded in our favour, for God is the supreme psychiatrist. He knows our weaknesses and pities our littleness, so that every mitigating circumstance will be taken into account. He is advocate as well as Judge, and it was to save us that He lived and died. But again there is one thing that He will not do—one thing which in a sense He cannot do. He will not save us in spite of ourselves.

I I
The Living God

The philosophers and metaphysicians tell us that God is eternal and unchangeable, that there is no composition in Him, and that He is all-knowing, all-powerful, and everywhere present; and the theologians, with their baffling precision of language, use terms like quiddity, pure act, and essence, which are too abstract for the rest of us. Yet we too must know God (for how can we love Him if we don't know Him?), so we speak of His infinite wisdom, goodness, and mercy, whittling down infinity to the grasp of our own finite intelligence, and, as Frank Sheed says somewhere, tending to think of God as "man writ large." Implied reproofs like this, however, need not depress us unduly, and the men on the bridge below the town may take comfort in the fact that the Curé d'Ars may have known more about God—and was no doubt a lot closer to Him—than the professors who had misgivings about his fitness for ordination.

Knowledge of God is not the monopoly of philosophers and theologians, for we are all indentured to it; and the way to it for most of us is not through study and discussion (though both have their place in the spiritual life). Knowledge of God is the gift of God, and the reward—as well as the reason—for loving and serving Him. "The man who loves me," says Christ, "is the man who keeps my commandments . . . I will love him, and will reveal myself to him." In these days, many theologians charge the Church with having conditioned men into believing that religion is no more than a set of commands and prohibitions (though the Church never did anything of the kind). If we love God, they say, everything else will follow. Christ said that too, but He said also that the man who really loves Him, and the man to whom He will reveal Himself, is the man who keeps His commandments. Knowledge of God grows in a climate of virtue, and it grows best in a climate of heroic virtue. Some of the saints—John of God and Teresa of Avila and Francis of Assisi—were especially favoured in this matter and in their ecstasies were vouchsafed glimpses of the Godhead which, though ravishing, were no more than premature, out-of-focus peeps at the curtained Beatific Vision. But for all of us, saints as well as sinners, getting to know God is a course that will last through all eternity; our heaven will not be spent twiddling our thumbs.

We must know God, and we must love Him too, but no sooner have we said, "O my God, I love Thee with all my strength and with all my mind" than we are filled with doubts. We wonder if we love God more than we love wife or husband, father or mother, and when we do we go right off beam. "It would be a grievous error," writes Dom Eugene Boylan (who as Kevin Boylan sat in the same class with me over fifty years ago), "to conceive the love of God as something which essentially involves sense-emotion or feeling. The love of God lies in the grace-aided will . . . A very high degree of love of God is quite compatible with an absence of emotion and even a feeling of distaste for the service of God . . . In fact, if one is going to achieve the heights of the spiritual life it is necessary to pass through a stage where one's apparent spiritual activity is reduced to a dry act of willingness to conform oneself to God's will."* This, coming from a master of the spiritual life, a Cistercian committed to penance and prayer and worship,

*This Tremendous Lover

78

should be a consolation to those who for long periods can achieve no more than this "dry act of willingness." Love of God is not just an emotion, though the emotions and the senses play their part in the spiritual life, and though we worship with our whole being. The love of God, as Boylan says tersely, lies in the "grace-aided will."

"You ask me," says St. Bernard, "for what reason and in what measure we should love God. I reply: 'The reason for loving God is God. The method and measure is to love Him without method or measure.' "* God has a lien on our love. He is the only thing worth loving, since all things other than God are loved in God. Once we accept this intellectually, and submit our wills to God (though with His help always, for love of God lies in the grace-aided will) we are loving Him. Feeling good or virtuous or exalted when we serve (which may mean no more than robust health or the anticipation of a good breakfast, and which is sometimes a subtle temptation) is beside the point, and we may get more merit from our prayers (and love God better) when going on our knees is a sore penance than when it seems as pleasant and natural as going for a swim. The thing that matters is whether we go on our knees, and our personal feelings are neither here nor there.

(I know of one convent—and believe that there are many such —where the nuns go to Mass on weekdays only when they feel like it. Their grandmothers, I suggest, were better theologians. These liberated religious would be the better for reading St. Teresa, and they would have got short shrift in her convent of the *Incarnación*, just outside the walls of Avila. And they are poor psychologists as well as poor theologians, for the will must be strengthened by effort and it is only by going against the grain that one builds up character—or spirituality.)

The burning love of God which St. John of the Cross expressed

On the Love of God

79

in his mystical and luminous verse was not born of the theology he learned in Salamanca but was the result of that dark night of the soul, that cumulative surrender of the self which was like a kind of death, leaving a void to be filled with a two-way circuit of love. The saints got in the measure of their giving; pressed down and flowing over. Moreover, their yielding up of the very citadel of personality strengthened its defences and involved growth rather than shrinking. The saints are more human than the rest of us; more integrated, more positive, more real. It is we, and not they, who are shadowy.

They learned to love God (and to know Him) the hard way, which is the only way; and they have much to teach us, for the truth (consoling or terrifying, according to how you look at it) is that we must all be saints or suffer the consequences. God alone knows how much is expected of each of us, and He will not be satisfied with less. The admonition "Be ye perfect" is for the many, not for the few, and God is not the one for half measures. "Heaven," Eugene Boylan says, "supposes perfect love of God, which must be reached in this life, or else, with far more suffering in the next through the fires of purgatory."* And we find the same thought in C. S. Lewis: "I will never rest, nor let you rest, until you are literally perfect—until my Father can say without reservation that he is well pleased with you, as he was well pleased with me. This much I can do and will do. But I will not do anything less."† God, as George MacDonald puts it, is easy to please but hard to satisfy.

To know Him, to love Him, and to serve Him: it's as simple as that—and as complex. But how can we, contingent, finite beings, know the transcendent, infinite God? The answer is that we can know Him—and love Him—in the measure that He vouchsafes

*This Tremendous Lover
†Beyond Personality

(since we can do nothing without Him); and we should not bother too much about the philosophical difficulty. The apostles were not scholars, but they knew God and listened to His words; and we can listen too, at one remove. The Incarnation, one might say, has made things easier, but in another sense it has made the problem more difficult and more baffling since it brings us right up against the mystery of the Trinity.

It was a long time before Christ revealed His divinity to His apostles (explicitly, that is, for He gave leads and pointers from the very beginning), and it was longer still before the Holy Spirit came into the picture. But we, with revelation to guide us, serve no such apprenticeship, and are journeymen from the moment we learn our first prayers. "In God there are three divine Persons," we are taught, "really distinct, and equal in all things—the Father, and the Son, and the Holy Ghost."

Strangely enough (though perhaps not so strangely, since faith is one of the fruits of baptism), this the most baffling of mysteries is accepted by us without question or puzzlement from our earliest years. Young children question the why and the wherefore of everything else, but they take the Trinity in their stride. Once they have learned that there are three Persons in God, and that though each is God there is only one God, it becomes as much of an axiom as the truth that the whole is greater than its parts—of which it seems a contradiction. Later they learn the corollaries—that the divine nature is not shared, that each of the three Persons possesses it in its entirety, knowing with the same intellect and loving with the same will—but still there is no questioning. Acceptance and unquestioning faith are their strong suits.

Acceptance and faith will serve for us too, but as adult Christians a little more is expected of us. We can never penetrate the mystery of the Trinity, but we must come to terms with it as best we can, because it is as the Trinity that the Godhead must be known and loved.

We can at least rid ourselves of some false notions, and the first false notion is that there is some hint of priority or precedence in the word "proceeds." For there is no question of priority or precedence, just as there is no question of seniority. The Son proceeds from the Father, but proceeds eternally; the Holy Spirit proceeds from the Father and the Son, but exists eternally with them.

But why three Persons? Three, because of the nature of the Godhead. The Father knows Himself, and His idea of Himself must utterly match and mirror the reality; otherwise He would have an inadequate knowledge of Himself; and the knowledge which the Father has of Himself, the "Word" that He utters, is equal to Him but distinct from Him, and being equal, not a something but a Someone. "In the beginning," says St. John, "was the Word, and the Word was with God, and the Word was God." From the beginning, too (the beginning that was no beginning), Father and Son loved one another with an infinite love; and this love, again, is not a something but a Someone. The Holy Spirit, the Third Person of the Trinity, proceeds from the Father and the Son as the utterance of their infinite love.

Knowing even this much about the Blessed Trinity we are still outside the mystery but we are no longer in complete darkness. There are faint glimmers of light, though an old peasant woman praying "In the name of the Father and of the Son and of the Holy Spirit" might still have a head start on us.

It is as the Trinity that the Godhead must be known and loved, and the fact that God is Father, Son, and Spirit is the basis of our theology. It is significant that this fundamental truth should have been stressed in a declaration issued by the Congregation of the Faith as recently as February, 1972. Old heresies seldom die, and the doctrine of the Trinity is one of the many dogmas of the Church which are being challenged in our own day in the name of the new theology. Shortly after the February declaration, Cardinal Danielou, speaking at a French Episcopal Conference, drew attention to Robert Michiels' questioning of the Trinitarian and Christological teaching of the Church in his *Jesus Christ—Yesterday, Today, and Tomorrow*. Drawing on the theologians of the Dutch school (many of whom, in the old days, would have been openly named as heretics), Michiels sees in Christ merely the man in whom God reveals Himself, and he quotes Schonnenberg to the effect that God "becomes" Trinitarian by sending Jesus and the Spirit. For him, Christ is a human person, nothing more, and the starting point of Christology is no longer the pre-existence of God's Word within the divinity but the unique—though human —character of the man Jesus. This may be theology of a sort, but one thing it is not: it is not Catholic theology.

The doctrine of the Trinity is not a plaything for speculative theologians. It is the basis of spirituality and faith, and it is as this that it is being challenged. It was almost as shrouded in mystery for Augustine and Duns Scotus as it is for the rest of us, but it is our duty—as it was theirs—to think about it once in a while, even if we never get beyond a statement of it which is neither sophisticated nor complex. "When one realises the infinite nature of God, his fullness of perfection, and at the same time the utter simplicity of his Being, one is not surprised to learn that the activity of his intellect and will should issue in images of him of such a richness and plenitude of likeness to their source that they are subsistent Persons within the sole Being of the Godhead."* Something more rigorous might be expected of a candidate submitting a thesis for his doctorate in theology, but anyone wishing merely to make the Sign of the Cross with more devotion and understanding would find enough in it for a lifetime of reflection.

*Joseph Faa Di Bruno: *Catholic Belief* (Cartmell)

12
The Human
Condition

What we think of the human condition depends on whether or not we believe with C. S. Lewis that after Adam's revolt "a new species sinned itself into existence," so that ever since there is a dichotomy in our nature, we are pulled both ways at once and have a fight on our hands. The alternative doctrine is that man is naturally good, that Adam is a biblical myth, that progress is continuous and inevitable, that the alleged downward drag in our nature is a fiction sponsored by the Church, and that ignorance and superstition are being swept away by the march of science and the spread of popular education.

Our treatment of prisoners, it is pointed out, is much more humane than it used to be (though there are disturbing rumours from Siberia), sheep-stealers are no longer hanged in public (though we may have to do something drastic very soon to put an end to the hijacking of planes), and the poor (who used to have the gospel preached to them) get free medical treatment (which John of God gave them four centuries ago). No one may ill-treat animals with impunity, and cruelty to children has been outlawed (though they may be evicted summarily from the womb and incinerated at the public expense). Physical suffering (the only real evil) is on the way out, the old and infirm are given state pensions or cared for in institutions (expenditure under this heading will be cut when euthanasia is introduced), and food, medicines, and clothing are rushed to faraway places as soon as disaster strikes.

It cannot be denied that there have been dramatic and cumulative improvements in social conditions in our time, but it does not follow either that there has been a corresponding improvement in human nature or that men are naturally good and are made evil only by outside influences, so that, given the right environmental conditions (which range from government restrictions on private property to the abolition of religious dogma and denominational schools) they show themselves as tolerant, kindly, good-natured, and brimming with brotherly love. This is a plausible theory, but it does not fit in with the facts.

Before we see the twentieth century as more enlightened and more humane than the centuries which dotted Europe with cathedrals, monastery schools, and almshouses, there is a little totting to be done on the debit side. Dachau and Auschwitz are recent memories, and the Russians, who with a show of virtuous indignation condemned Stalin's purges, showed little scruple in crushing revolts in Poland, Hungary, and East Germany; murder for the heck of it is a modern development, and the punishing of people for the political defection of near relatives, which is a commonplace behind the Iron Curtain, is a refinement for which we can find no parallel during the long centuries when Europe and Christendom were synonymous. The history of the twentieth century, far from proving that humanity is being gradually shorn of evil and that the spirit of brotherhood is burgeoning everywhere, provides evidence of a sick civilization and of a secular ethic from which the old moral values of Christianity are being erased one by one.

It will be argued that cruelty is now universally condemned, and that Hitler's name will be execrated for ever; but it was twentieth-century men who herded the Jews into Hitler's gas chambers, and the murder of 15,000 Polish officers, priests, and scholars by the Russians at Katyn Forest was a twentieth-century crime. Nor is the world's condemnation of cruelty as universal as one might think, for expediency and selective indignation play a part in it. Hitler has a place in the Rogues' Gallery, but Chairman Mao has his place at the United Nations and visiting heads of state have no qualms about shaking his bloody hand.

It will be argued too that the crimes of totalitarian regimes are the crimes of the few, and that "ordinary" people the world over are and have always been kindly, neighbourly, law-abiding folk whose only wish is to live at peace and rear their families. You and I, for example. We are model citizens. We keep the law and harm no one. We love our children and are loyal to our friends. We help blind men across the street and send flowers to the sick, and our subscriptions to charity are not much short of our golf subscriptions. We have no police record, and no one can point a finger at us. (Publicly, that is, for there was someone, long ago, who wrote with His finger in the sand.)

How we would measure up to Pascal's test is another matter; for Pascal said that there are only two kinds of people: the sinners, who think themselves righteous, and the righteous, who think themselves sinners. Our complacency may well be a proof that we have no cause for complacency, and it might crumble if we contrasted the reality (which we hide sometimes even from ourselves) with the image which we project.

If things have gone wrong in the world—and in spite of our vaunted humanitarianism they have gone badly wrong—the fault lies not with the big sinners but with the little ones; for if "ordinary" Christians were all as good as they should be (which means as good as God wants them to be) the world would be set right overnight. But most of us are content to be as good as the next (who may be better than he seems), to keep some of the rules some of the time, and to comfort ourselves with the thought that we measure up to a fictitious average which, granted the beam in our own eye, is adjusted in our favour. And that is not what God asks of us; what God asks of us is perfection, and the amount by which we fall short of perfection is the measure of our failure.

Each of our personal struggles is part of a bigger struggle—the vast interlocking struggle of good and evil that will last until the end of time. Each one of us, at every moment of life, is making the world better or worse; and the real tragedy is, not that there are so many who are sold and committed to evil, but that there are so few who are sold and committed to good. Saints are always in short supply.

Holiness—not heroic holiness but ordinary common or garden holiness, which links love of one's neighbour with love of God (and there are some people whom it would not be easy to love except for Christ's sake)—begins with a hard look at the self. "As the light grows," says Fenélon, "we see ourselves to be worse than we thought. We are amazed at our former blindness, and we see issuing from our hearts a whole swarm of shameful feelings like reptiles crawling from a hidden cave. But we must not be disturbed. We are not worse than we thought; on the contrary, we are better."

Fenélon's language is more suited to the pulpits of the seventeenth century than to the seminars of the twentieth, but Newman says much the same thing when he stresses the importance of a "self-abased, self-renouncing heart" as the basis of spiritual advancement. "All teaching about duty and obedience," he writes, "about attaining heaven and the office of Christ towards us, is hollow and unsubstantial when it is not built *here*, in the doctrine of our original corruption and helplessness: and, in consequence, of original guilt and sin. Christ himself, indeed, is the foundation, but a broken, self-abased, self-renouncing heart is (as it were) the ground and soil in which the foundation must be laid."* Words like "corruption" and "helplessness" are out of fashion nowadays, but a realisation of their abiding significance will always have a place in any evaluation of our human condition.

Parochial and Plain Sermons, V, 134–5

One thing that often wearies rather than edifies us in the writings of the saints is their constant avowals of wretchedness and worthlessness, and when we find Teresa of Avila saying that God never granted her any outstanding favour except when she was "overcome with shame at the thought of her own wickedness" the temptation is to take the whole thing with a grain of salt. But Teresa was no sanctimonious *poseuse* striking an attitude, and she was certainly not a neurotic. In spite of her raptures her feet remained on solid earth, and her sturdy common sense was matched by an astringent sense of humour. Moreover she is a Doctor of the Church—an honour which is as much a tribute to her grasp of theological truth as to her sanctity and which is not achieved by way of hallucinations or hysterical imaginings.

Then there is the story of St. John of God who, when he was charged before the Archbishop with harbouring evil men in his hospital at Granada, threw himself on his knees and admitted that the charge was only too true, since he himself lived at the hospital. To us this may seem either simple-mindedness or subtle ploy, but it was neither. It was the humility and clear-sightedness of a saint. John had two standards, one for himself and one for his neighbour. He was merciless on himself; everyone else got the benefit of the doubt.

The humility of the saints, who were aware of—and many of whom chronicled—the extraordinary favours which God granted them, might seem an inverted pride, a "see how humble I am in spite of my holiness" pose, but it was utterly real and utterly rational; it was an acknowledgement of the truth that we have nothing of our own, that all God's gifts to us are gratuitous and undeserved, and that even our correspondence with His grace is as much a gift as the grace itself, since we can do nothing without His help.

Seeing man as he really is involves some idea first of both the grandeur and the limitations of his intellect and then of his place in creation. He is made in God's image and likeness, and has a rational soul with its powers of will and intellect. He rules over the animal world, the earth is his inheritance, and he is learning to tackle more and more of the problems which his overlordship poses for him. His knowledge is growing all the time, and prophets like Nietzsche and Chardin look for the arrival of the superman before the story is finished.

No wonder, then, that our achievements tend to go to our heads —though we work with donated intellectual tools and are as limited as regards materials as a child with a Meccano set. "What a piece of work is man!" says Shakespeare. "How like an angel." How unlike, rather. For an angel has not to learn things in painful stages as we have, nor to reap where others have ploughed. His knowledge is instant and forever, and he is free from false leads and fumblings. Aquinas was called the Angelic Doctor, but he had to work for his knowledge like the rest of us, and he was a lumbering carthorse compared with Michael or Gabriel. (Though how he will rate when he gets his glorified body is anyone's guess.)

We can think of one or two things at a time, but only a tithe of our knowledge is in focus at any instant, and, unlike the angels, we cannot survey the whole field at once. (Someone will tell me now that angels are out, that the Scriptures have been thoroughly demythologised, and that today's priests, when they have celebrated Mass, do not beg Michael to thrust Satan down to hell and with him all the other wicked spirits who wander through the world for the ruin of souls. But the demythologisers will soon be a spent force, and Michael's sword is still unsheathed.) We can bump our heads against the farthest stars, but our thoughts cannot gallop off wildly in all directions (like Leacock's man on the horse), and when we are busy at differential calculus the light is out for Chopin's preludes and the latest prices on the Stock Exchange.

We are mighty fine fellows, but we have to learn and re-learn, and the sieve of memory has wide meshes. Duns Scotus was better than most of us, but only relatively, and the ratio of Einstein's mental equipment to that of anyone who can count his chickens and link cause and effect is only a shade greater than unity.

Whenever we have delusions of grandeur, either because of our own individual gifts or the bulked achievements of our race, it will cool our heads to think of the angels and angelic knowledge—so long as we remember that they, like ourselves, are indebted to God for all that they have. It would be well to remember too that in spite of their shining gifts we can still outface them; for one of us was the Son of God, and we are all adopted children of His Mother.

13
The Fall

The belief that the entire human race is descended from one pair of ancestors and that our myriad family trees arrow back to and converge on a man called Adam is not—to put it mildly—as widely held as it used to be. It was once an axiom of faith for all Christians, but in these days it is derided as a myth which satisfied our ignorant forbears (including such intellectual minnows as Thomas More and Bonaventure), but which twentieth-century man, nurtured on Darwin and Teilhard, cannot be expected to swallow. The ignorant and credulous centuries had to be given some account of man's origin and lineage, and the biblical myth served a purpose until people became sophisticated enough to accept the theory of evolution. The result is that, nowadays, any school child with a smattering of biology, topped up with the new catechetics, knows that Adam and Eve belong with Santa Claus and Sleeping Beauty and the other innocuous fables which satisfied the people of God in the dark days before television.

The Church's attitude to all this, as I have already pointed out, is at once accommodating and strict, and Catholics are free to believe that the human body derived from lower forms of matter. But they must also believe that our rational souls did not evolve but are directly created by God, and in that disorder in our nature known as original sin; and any attempt to reconcile these three beliefs leads to formidable intellectual difficulties.

Even Teilhard admitted this. The impossibility of reconciling his own beliefs with the Church's teaching did not worry him unduly, but he had the grace to feel some misgivings, and this much must be credited to him. "I am sometimes a little frightened," he wrote in 1922, "when I think of the transposition to which I must subject the common notions of creation, inspiration, miracle, original sin, etc., in order to accept them."*

He was not always frightened, however—only sometimes; and he was only a little frightened—when as a Catholic priest he should have been panicked. Moreover, he had already begun to tamper with the fundamental doctrines which he belittles as "common notions," since as well as seeing no place for original sin in his all-embracing concept he saw evil, not as the result of disobedience to God's laws, but as an inevitable by-product of the evolutionary process "relentlessly imposed by the play of large numbers at the heart of a multitude undergoing organization"; and the Incarnation as Christ, "the principle of universal vitality," putting Himself into the position (maintained ever since) to subdue unto himself, to direct and superanimate, the general ascent of consciousness into which he inserted Himself.† This mind-numbing juggling with words and phrases so imprecise that their meaning is anyone's guess is far removed from the strenuous discipline of reasoned argument. It is also far removed from the basic truth that Christ became man to redeem and save us; and Dietrich von Hildebrand does not exaggerate when he charges Teilhard with "utter theological confusion."** The only way in which the basic doctrines which Teilhard questions could be brought into line with his Gnostic notions would be to rewrite the whole deposit of faith.

The arrival of the first man, even assuming that his physical

*Lettres, Grasset, Paris (1962)
† The Phenomenon of Man
** The Trojan Horse in the City of God

body evolved, was not a mutation, or the final stage in a long progression. It marked the birth of thought and reason, and to speak of thought as something generated little by little in the womb of animal consciousness is to libel the mighty men who, in the dark morning of our race, struck sparks from flint—using the same God-given reason which, in time, enabled their successors to dream up the computer. The first man was not a new step in the argument; he was not part of the argument at all. All that went before was merely the decor, the scenery, the setting. Now the first actor had made his appearance, and the play was about to begin. The pseudo-scientific magazines which appear in fortnightly parts (binders available) present our remote ancestors as fumbling, dim-witted creatures, but the truth is that the first men were as well equipped intellectually as those who in due course were to write concertos and establish bridgeheads on the moon.

Man had no infancy ("thousands of years," Teilhard tells us). The first man was an adult from the very beginning, so that much that we have to learn by trial and error was his from the first moment of his existence. His one disadvantage, compared with us, was that he had no reservoir of experience to draw on, no ancestors to bequeath him an inheritance of factual knowledge. With this solitary exception the advantages were all on his side.

Until they fell, Adam and Eve strode the earth like gods. They could meet with no accident, suffer no hurt; and death had no dominion over them; when their time came, they would simply, by a pleasant and painless transition, exchange a temporary lodging for a permanent one and go straight to God. They were ruled by reason, and their passions never strained against the leash. There was no clash of concupiscence and conscience in them. Their wills, though utterly free, were directed and orientated towards their Creator. When they sinned, they sinned with perfect knowledge and full consent; and their punishment was summary and instant.

Adam was not only the first man, but the prototype of all men;

and so the special gifts which he enjoyed were lost for all who came after him. "The Fall," as C. S. Lewis says, "was loss of status as a species." The result was that forever after—inevitably and inescapably—every man and woman born by way of carnal generation, with the single exception of the Mother of God, lacked the privileges which Adam enjoyed and by virtue of which all his powers and faculties acted always in perfect harmony with each other and in complete conformity to the will of God.

For Adam, it was a changed world. The stone chafed his heel, the nettle stung him, and the cobra lay in wait. His understanding dimmed, his will weakened, and there was in him, as the old Catechism put it, "a strong inclination to evil." Once he had been master in his own house. Now the price of virtue was eternal vigilance. His God-given integrity—the right relation of soul and body, of the spiritual and the material—was sundered forever. The curse had come upon him.

But after the curse came the promise, and God made a new contract with man. His sovereignty was pared and trimmed, but it was still sovereignty. He was still the King's son, and there was a place for him in his Father's house. But the terms of the lease had been revised, and his estate was no longer a freehold. The weeds could choke his harvest, the winds scatter his thatch, the rain quench his fire; and work, which had once been as much of a delight as the rest that followed it, was now a penance and a burden. He had to earn his bread by the sweat of his brow, and he had to die the death.

But why should we suffer with Adam? And how can every child, long before he is capable of sinning, and even from the very instant of his conception, be cited as co-defendant with a remote ancestor? How can that doctrine be reconciled with the concept of a just and merciful God? Eve ate the apple; why should we get the stomachache?

The answer is that we share, not in Adam's sin, but—and of

necessity—in its consequences. Adam, had he remained faithful, would have founded a race of men like himself, since the special gifts with which God endowed him were potential family traits; but when he sinned he handed on his own damaged nature. It was the only nature he *could* hand on. Adam was a changed man, and he perpetuated his kind.

Moreover, although we lost much by Adam's sin, we gained more than we lost; for God the Son became man (the words of the old Catechism keep coming back) "to redeem and save us," not just to redeem and save Adam. He became one of us (one of this new species which had sinned itself into existence), taking a created body and a created soul (both of which were created at a definite point in time—a tremendous truth which we often forget), atoning by His passion and death for all the sins of mankind, and offering to His Father on our behalf the only fit and acceptable appeasement for our bulked treasons and disloyalties. And here surely was gain beyond all measure, so that the *felix culpa* of the Easter liturgy is not poetic licence but solid truth; for Adam's sin has brought us an unmerited grace, and in the heavenly accountancy the impoverishment that we speak of as "original sin" is an asset beyond all computation.

And it is dangerously easy to exaggerate this impoverishment, real and substantial though it is. We are poor, admittedly, but we are also immeasurably rich in that, through Christ, we have a claim on the Father. We sometimes say that Christ "humbled Himself for our humanity," but this is a figure of speech; for God cannot humble Himself or lessen His majesty, and it might be nearer the truth to say that God the Son, in becoming man, exalted humanity and gave a new dimension to the human condition.

To see the Fall in perspective we must see the passion and death of Christ as the central point of the divine plan; Christ, of whose fullness we have all received, and who, as Abbot Marmion says, "is not only holy in himself but is *our* holiness"; Christ, because of whom we are all sons of God by adoption. Christ is God's infinite gift to us, and the gifts which Adam lost for us by his sin are as nothing in comparison. Christ, as St. Paul says in the Epistle to the Hebrews, "is always living to make intercession for us," and the Eden episode is not simply a dark chapter in the history of our race but the eternally foreseen prelude to the coming of the Redeemer.

The Fall rationalizes and explains the dichotomy that is in every one of us: the clash of loyalties, the shame and the glory, the tug this way and that. Modern psychology (and not a few modern theologians are trimming their sails accordingly) sees evil in terms of anti-social tendencies which are the result of glandular secretions and environmental and hereditary influences, and teaches that we are what we are by necessity rather than choice; but to deny the existence of evil in the sense of something which we may either choose or reject is to go against experience, for each of us is aware of the evil in himself and is conscious of the presence of tendencies which, though strong, are never irresistible unless by our own volition we let them become so and deliberately pass the point of no return. Each of us knows that he is not good or bad as a permanent condition, but good at one time and bad at another according as he resists or gives way.

This duality raises a question to which, if we reject the doctrine of the Fall, there is no satisfactory answer. "It is an astonishing fact," says Pascal, "that the mystery furthest removed from our comprehension, namely the transmission of sin, is one without which we can have no understanding of ourselves. Nothing affronts our reason more deeply than this doctrine, and yet without it we remain incomprehensible. The secret of our human nature twists and turns in this abyss, and man is more inconceivable without the mystery than the mystery is inconceivable to man."*

*Pensées

98

This has been endorsed by C.E.M. Joad in our own day, and the quoted source* adds something to the weight of his testimony. "I see now," he wrote, "that evil is endemic in man, and that the Christian doctrine of original sin expresses a deep and essential insight into human nature. Reject it and you fall victim, as so many of us whose minds have developed in an atmosphere of left-wing politics and rationalist philosophy, to a shallow optimism in regard to human nature which causes you to think that the millenium is just round the corner waiting to be introduced by a society of perfectly psychoanalysed, prosperous Communists."

The doctrine of original sin makes sense of the human story, and Joad's "shallow optimism" has come a terrible cropper in our time. Improved social conditions, better education, and the cumulative lessening of the gap between the haves and the have nots have done little to increase our moral stature, and material prosperity has not made us better men and women. The naive belief that a more equitable sharing of wealth would in itself ensure a better and a kindlier world is a brittle philosophy, and the vague and selective humanitarianism to which it leads crumples under the pressure of selfishness and greed. Moreover it leaves an unsolved, nagging question, with drugs and eroticism as the only escape hatch—the Jekyll-and-Hyde enigma that is each of us. Seen in the light of the Fall, the enigma vanishes; and the Redemption fits all the pieces into place.

*Rationalist Annual, 1946

14

The Mother
of God

The honour which we Catholics pay to the Mother of God has lost us many friends, and in spite of our continuing explanations (for we make no apologies) it is still widely regarded as only this side of idolatry. We are patient when our critics say that we give Mary too much honour, but we have no patience whatever when we are accused of giving her divine honour; for if there is one truth that is drummed and dinned into every Catholic child from his earliest years it is the nature of the honour that we give to Mary. "We honour the Blessed Virgin more than all the other saints," we learn when we are still lisping our numbers, "because Christ himself so much honoured her, but we never give her supreme or divine honour, which is due to God alone." And Christ certainly did honour her; He picked her as His mother.

It is suggested too that the honour we pay to Mary is a potential danger for ill-instructed Catholics, though if there are any Catholics who do not grasp the gulf that separates the Creator from His creatures they could scarcely be described even as deists. The truth is that it is not the ignorant, or the young, or the badly-instructed, who fail to grasp the nature of the honour we pay to the Mother of God; and this can be easily proved by testing a sampling of them. It is the professors, not the peasants, who have gone off the track, and some of our latter-day theologians who think that we might win over our separated brethren more easily if we played down the importance of Mary in God's plan for the world give more scandal to those they are trying to bring into the fold than do the peasant women who carry lighted candles in processions.

The Catholic attitude to Mary is summed up in the words of St. Louis de Montfort, who was a tireless—almost a fanatical—servant of the Mother of God, who based his spirituality on her, and who spent his life spreading devotion to her. "I avow with the Church," he writes, "that Mary, being but a mere creature who has come from the hands of the All-High, is, in comparison with His infinite majesty, less than an atom, or rather, she is nothing at all." Once it is conceded that this is what every Catholic believes, and what every Catholic child is taught over and over again, we are willing to continue the discussion; but if the charge is that any Catholic, even the most badly-instructed, believes or is in danger of believing that Mary does not stand with the rest of us on one side of the abyss that separates us from our Creator, then all we can do is change the subject.

Why do we honour Mary? We honour Mary because she is the mother not just of Christ's human nature (for a mother does not give birth to a nature) but of the Second Person of the Blessed Trinity. Christ had no human personality—it was the only human attribute that He lacked—and once we admit that Mary was His mother the rest follows. Mary is more closely linked with the Godhead (whilst remaining infinitely distant from it) than any other creature, since by the power of the Holy Ghost she had the unspeakable privilege of being associated with the Father in the human birth of the Son. This is what sets her apart from all other creatures; this is why she is blessed among women. God the Son, the Second Person of the Blessed Trinity, took a human soul and a human body; and He had a human mother, who was the purest of creatures and the glory of her kind.

We address Mary by many titles, calling her Queen of Prophets and Queen of Patriarchs, Queen of Confessors and Queen of

Martyrs. We also address her as Queen of Angels, and although this is a microscopic honour compared to her glory as the Mother of God, it is worth reflecting on. The angels shine like stars, but Mary dazzles them. (We would do well to remember, too, that she is our mother as well as God's—He shared her with us when we nailed Him up.)

Two things make Gabriel's message to Mary breathtaking. The first is that he came, not to command in God's name, but to announce a plan that depended—quite literally—on Mary's consent; and the second is that he addressed her as "full of grace." He knelt before Mary, and he knelt because he knew that there was no flaw in her, because in Mary grace was packed down and flowing over.

Only once, in the *Magnificat*, did Mary speak in character. It is an incomparable poem, and it had no successor. It said all that Mary had to say. The Almighty had done great things to her; she was His handmaid, and her spirit rejoiced. After that, so far as the record goes—silence, except when she showed her confidence and her power at Cana.

They must have had many conversations, these two—Mother and Son, creature and Creator—but Mary kept her secret to the end. During His public life she was always, as far as the Gospel story goes, a background figure, but she was a coadjutress and not just a spectator. She helped to carry the Cross, and made the carrying of it heavier because the sight of her suffering increased her Son's suffering. Her martyrdom mingled with His. And He ceded her to mankind almost with His last breath. She was His parting gift, and in giving it He brought us all into the Holy Family.

The protests that greeted the proclamation of the dogma of the Assumption—and the echoes have not died away yet—are difficult to understand. "If we believe in the resurrection of the body," as C.E.M. Joad said once with merciless logic, "how can we reject

the Assumption, which was merely doing earlier for Mary something which will be done for every one of us later, and therefore
not an unthinkable compliment for the Son of God to pay to His
Mother?" The proclamation of the dogma, moreover, did not lay
down a new article of faith but merely endorsed a truth which
Catholics had always accepted, and which was based on reason as
well as reverence. Death is a punishment for sin, and Mary was
sinless from the moment of her conception. There was no concupiscence in her, and it is unthinkable that her virginal flesh, from
which Christ's own flesh was formed, should suffer the indignity
of decay and putrefaction.

There are some who would degrade Mary to the status of a
biological necessity; but Christ, who had no human father, could
just as easily have had no human mother. But he *had* a human
mother. He chose her and fashioned her and made her blessed
among women.

Mary was saluted by Gabriel as "full of grace," but her grace was
not absolute. She grew in holiness all through her life, and Pope
Pius IX, in his definition of the Immaculate Conception, referred
to her as "forever increasing her original gift." But all holiness,
even Mary's, is a response as well as a gift, and she who was
destined to become the Mother of God had to be asked. Her
consent was a necessary prelude to the divine drama; and if she
knew the script before consenting to play the lead she must have
been not only the purest of creatures but a better theologian than
Aquinas.

There are only two views open to us: one is that Mary played
—and continues to play—a key role in God's plan for the world;
the other is that she was no more than a human instrument whose
function was completed when she had borne her Child. The first
is part of the enduring Christian tradition, and in every age it has
enabled untold thousands to see Mary as the sure way to her Son;
the second is the seed bed of heresies, and it clashes with both the

beginning and the end of the scriptural story of our redemption; for the beginning was the message of Gabriel, and the end was the words which Christ spoke to St. John from the Cross.

Christ's words to John were a codicil to His last will and testament. He had already committed His Church to the care and guardianship of the apostles; now He was committing the Church and the apostles—and not just the hierarchical Church but also the Church as the People of God—to the care of His Mother. Mary was the Mother of Christ's human body. She is also, and to the end of time, the Mother of the Church, His Mystical Body; and in the Upper Room, when the Holy Spirit descended on the infant Church, she was there "to preside over the birth of this new Humanity."*

Mary was silent for most of her life, but during the last century and a half she has spoken often: notably at the Rue de Bac, Paris (1830), La Salette (1846), Lourdes (1858), and Fatima (1917). To the modern mind, the mention of apparitions smacks of superstition and medieval credulity (though spiritualism is quite respectable), and many of our latter-day ecumenists would gladly dismantle all the shrines; but whilst it is one thing to discount the apparitions, it is quite another to discount the evidence adduced in support of them. Facts are facts, and the phenomenon of the gyrating sun at Fatima is as authentic a piece of history as the sinking of the *Titanic*.

On six occasions between May and October, 1917, the Blessed Virgin appeared to three Portuguese children aged seven, nine, and ten. The first apparition occured on 13 May, and on Our Lady's instructions the children returned to the scene on the thirteenth of each succeeding month. If men did penance, she told them (and much else besides), Russia would be converted. Otherwise Russia would spread her errors throughout the world. But in

*Father James, O.F.M.Cap.: *How to Say the Rosary*

the end her Immaculate Heart would triumph, and peace would reign.

At the July apparition, Our Lady, the children said, told them that on 13 October she would reveal her identity and work a great miracle "so that all may believe." On 13 October a crowd of about 100,000 people accompanied the children to the scene of the apparitions. Our Lady announced herself as the Queen of the Rosary, said that a church should be built at the spot in her honour, and warned that men must not continue to offend God, who had already been offended too much.

The crowd saw or heard nothing of all this, but they all saw what followed. The sun shone out suddenly in what had been until then a dark and clouded sky, whirled like a gigantic fire-wheel, and sent out streamers of green, red, orange, and purple which lit up the faces of the multitude. Then, gyrating madly, it plunged precipitately, before rising again in a zigzag path to its original position.

One of the most striking accounts of this amply-attested phenomenon is that given by Avelino de Almeida, editor of Lisbon's biggest daily, who only the day before had published an article discounting the apparitions and sneering at the credulous peasants "whom the miraculous still attracts, seduces, bewitches, consoles, and fortifies." De Almeida's account of the spectacle is long and detailed, and he speaks of it as "unique and incredible if one had not been a witness of it."

And what of the three children themselves? Could they, in view of their youth and lack of sophistication, have invented the messages they claimed to have received from Our Lady? Then they must have been briefed and brainwashed by people who planned the whole fraud in advance and who, as Senhor de Almeida suggested in his 12 October article, dreamed of a new place of pilgrimage to rival Lourdes and bring prosperity to the whole district. If so they must have been very remarkable children, since during the period of the apparitions they were ridiculed by everyone, even by

106

their own families. Moreover, like Bernadette, they were interrogated and re-interrogated, threatened, and imprisoned, yet they remained clear and unconfused and there was absolute uniformity in the stories they told, despite the fact that the *content* of Our Lady's messages (of which I have given only a brief and incomplete summary) was of a complexity that cannot be reconciled with their education and background.

Must a Catholic believe in the apparitions and messages of Fatima? No, because they were private revelations. (He may even shrug off the demented gyrations of the sun, in spite of the testimony of thousands of witnesses, many of whom were as hostile initially as Senhor de Almeida.) All the Church says of the Fatima revelations is that they are "worthy of credence." (The world, of course, says nothing at all. The mystery of the *Marie Celeste* crops up every five years or so, but Fatima is ignored by a generation that demands signs and wonders.) On the other hand, all the Popes from Benedict XV to Paul VI have been devoted to Fatima, its church has been elevated to the rank of a minor basilica, and Pope John XXIII willed his pectoral cross to its shrine.

The story of Lourdes has been well chronicled, and *The Song of Bernadette* has gone round the world, but the apparition at La Salette, the shrine on the slopes of the Alps, is not as well known as it should be, though it preceded those of Lourdes and Fatima and was a prelude to them, for each of Mary's visits is part of her pleading.

"The apparition at La Salette," writes Jacques Maritain, "is one of the most important events that have taken place for centuries." Maritain and his wife Raïssa became interested in La Salette through their friend Léon Bloy, whose devotion to Our Lady was a cornerstone of his spirituality. A struggling writer, who seldom earned enough to keep his family and who knew pawnshop poverty all his life, Bloy was tireless in defending the Church and in spreading devotion to La Salette. "I spend part of my days," he

107

wrote once, "at the feet of a Jewess whose slave I am and whose heart is transpierced."

In outline, the story of the apparition of La Salette is briefer and less complex than that of either Lourdes or Fatima. Only two children were involved, and Our Lady made only one appearance, which lasted about half an hour. Nor did she reveal her identity explicitly. To the children she was merely "the Beautiful Lady."

She was enveloped, the children said, in a whirling globe of light, which they entered when she called to them. "Come here, children," she said. "Do not be afraid." Her face was buried in her hands, her elbows rested on her knees, and tears flowed down her cheeks as she spoke.

"If my people will not submit," she told them, "I shall be forced to let fall the arm of my Son. It is so strong, so heavy, that I cannot withhold it. So long do I suffer for you! If I would not have my Son abandon you I am compelled to pray without ceasing. However much you pray, however much you do, you will never recompense the pains I have taken for you."

She went on to enumerate the many ways in which men were offending her Son, and she ended by telling the children to "make this known to all my people." But her tears were even more moving and more terrifying than her words. Bloy, in his book *Celle Qui Pleure (She Who Weeps)*, describes the Discourse of La Salette as "the most doleful sigh heard since the *Consummatum*"; and Cardinal Fornari said of it: "I am frightened by such prodigies. When heaven has recourse to means like these, the need must be appalling."

As in the case of Fatima, the content of Our Lady's La Salette message was such that invention and planned deceit would be beyond the powers of even the most precocious children of this age (eleven and fourteen), and these, it must be remembered, were children from a remote rural area. Moreover, there were no discrepancies in their separate accounts of what Our Lady had said

108

(which they repeated time and time again), and their descriptions of her clothes were remarkable for their detail.

Five years later, in December, 1851, the Bishop of Grenoble issued a Mandate declaring that the apparition of La Salette "bore all the evidence of truth" and that the grounds for believing in it were "indubitable and certain." The following year, when laying the foundation stone for the shrine on the Holy Mountain, he announced the formation of the Missionary Order of La Salette, which was granted Roman rights and privileges in 1879 and is now worldwide, with several flourishing foundations in the United States.

Our Lady's periodic appearances and her repeated warnings are discounted by many of our latter-day theologians, who make recurring apologies for their superstitious fellow-Catholics and complain that any mention of apparitions or heavenly messages embarrasses them before the non-Catholic churchmen with whom they hold innocuous dialogues and theological get-togethers at which Catholic apologies are more noticeable than Catholic apologetics. It might do these common-denominator-seekers a world of good to reflect a little on the text "Son, behold thy Mother," which, if it was no more than an admonition to ensure that Our Lady's material wants would be provided for, would scarcely have merited a place in Christ's last tortured words from the Cross.

The truth is that Christ left us His Mother as our advocate and mediatrix, that we are still in need of her influence and intercession, and that devotion to her, as our Mother and His, is part of our heritage.* If those who are embarrassed by the apparitions

---

*Father Philip Hughes tells in his *Popular History of the Catholic Church* that although Catholicism in Japan was wiped out by persecution in the early seventeenth century, the first batch of missionaries admitted in 1865 found some 30,000 Catholics whose ancestors had kept the faith—without priests and without any sacraments but baptism—for over 200 years. And the Japanese Catholics recognised the missionaries as Catholics like themselves by three things: their acknowledgement of the authority of the pope; clerical celibacy; and devotion to the Mother of God.

wish to play them down they most go further and scrub out many of Our Lady's titles—Help of Christians, Comforter of the Afflicted, Refuge of Sinners, and Queen of Prophets; for when did she show herself as help, comforter, refuge, and prophet if not in her periodic visits to urge her people to penance and warn them of the consequences of their sins? And if the embarrassed ones still pray, "Turn then, O most gracious advocate, thine eyes of mercy towards us" (and even the most concession-minded ecumenists, one hopes—though it is only a hope—would draw the line at jettisoning the *Salve Regina*) they might think once in a while of La Salette, where the eyes of the most gracious advocate brimmed with mercy and compassion.

The apparitions bring Our Lady into sharper focus. During her earthly life her place was in the background. We are aware of her presence, and at Cana we have a proof of her power, but from the Finding in the Temple until the Crucifixion she is a shadowy, rarefied figure, totally absorbed by and immersed in her own interior life. But at La Salette and Lourdes and Fatima (though her appearances were by no means limited to these three places) she reveals herself as more motherly than any earthly mother; concerned, loving, tender-hearted; *alive* too—she who passed at once from earthly life to eternal life. She gives us fresh proof of her power with her divine Son, whose arm she withholds, and of her role as mediatrix and advocate. Mary, who was the Mother of Christ's human body, remains to the end of time the Mother of His Mystical Body, and as Father James says, when the Holy Spirit descended on the apostles in the Upper Room, she was there to preside over the birth of this new Humanity.

15

The Pilgrim Church

One fundamental misconception to which the committed Catholic is prone, especially in times when the Church is meeting with heavy weather (and tribulation, we should remember, is her legacy), is to think of "God's plan for the world" in much the same way as he thinks of Caesar's tactics or Napoleon's strategy, and to see Adam's fall as an event which changed the human story as God had originally written it. But to think that the whole sorry boiling of us from Adam to the last man to come from his mother's womb could put a spoke in God's wheel is badly muddled thinking. The mess that the angels made of things, the mess that men past, present, and to come have made, are making, or will make of things—all these have a place in a reckoning that was complete before anything but God was. Things always go God's way, for the simple reason that there is no other way they can go, and all that happens tends ultimately towards His glory and our good.

Nevertheless there are times when we must lean heavily on faith and trust, times when vice and corruption seem to be winning every trick, and when the Church herself seems to be fighting a losing battle. We have to remind ourselves then that although Christ guaranteed victory to His Church He did not promise an easy victory. The Pilgrim Church has to struggle; the Church Militant has to fight, and often against what seem insuperable odds.

And the odds against her have seldom seemed so formidable as in the years following Vatican II; not because the attacks are heavier, more frequent, or more sustained (though they are all of these), nor because humanists and Communists have made common cause against her, but because the strongest and most disheartening attacks come from the fifth column within. There was a time when the Church spoke with one voice; now many of her own priests and prelates charge her with being behind the times, with adhering stubbornly to anachronistic doctrines, and with insisting on an outdated moral code which must be revised drastically if the whole structure is not to disintegrate. The new overnight theologians challenge almost every ruling of the Magisterium; and, thanks to their grip on the mass media, their treasons become world news. The Church, they say, must compromise with the humanist views on sexual morality, make common cause with revolutionaries everywhere, come to terms with the Marxists (there are even "Catholic Marxists" nowadays), and see social betterment as the core and centre of Christ's teaching. She must stop unsettling young minds by talking of sin, hell, penance, self-denial, and mortification. And the time for doing all this is now. If she does not make concessions she will soon be out of business.

She must allow men and women to decide for themselves in everything that concerns the marriage bed, change her attitude to divorce, and introduce "optional celibacy" so that her priests may attain "self-fulfilment" and not take psychological hurt through repressing their sex instincts. (The priests of old, it may be mentioned in passing, achieved self-fulfilment the hard way, and were not noticeably neurotic.) Luther, as Maritain points out, was more open and more brutally honest. "Just as it is not within my power not to be a man," he declared, "it does not depend on me that I cannot live without a woman."*

* Three Reformers

Along with the demand for optional celibacy have come innovations which make it more difficult for religious to live up to their vows. "Co-educational seminaries, offensively dressed priests, charm courses for nuns, the public discussion by both of psychological problems arising from sexual repression, the indiscriminate mixing of ecclesiastics with crowds of the least inhibited—these are the channels through which the senses may be provoked and the boundary line between licit and illicit erased."* The celibacy issue is not a thing apart. It has obvious links with the new permissive society, and it is no accident that it has come to the forefront at this particular moment of time.

The sixteenth-century reformers appealed to the Scriptures as the sole guide in matters of faith and morals; the new go one better —they sieve the Scriptures, carry individual interpretation to manic depths, and dismiss as myth anything which they cannot reconcile with their Gnostic pontifying. Reunion is seen, not as the return of the separated churches, but as the establishment of a loose consortium after the liquidation of dogmatic differences. The yielding, however, must be all on the Catholic side, and amongst the truths which the new theologians question, deny, or are embarrassed by are the Real Presence of Christ in the Eucharist, the Virgin Birth, and the Resurrection. Devotion to the saints, novenas, and rosary beads are downgraded as superstitious survivals; belief in angels, original sin, and eternal punishment is regarded as no longer intellectually respectable; and the distinction between the Church teaching and the Church taught is blurred by constant reference to the authority of the "People of God" (as if this were a new concept dreamed up by Vatican II), co-responsibility, and the urgent need for a "democratization" of the Church.

The Reformation is seen as a tragic misunderstanding, all the

*Thomas Molnar, *Ecumenism or New Reformation?*

blame being put on the Church. Calvin, Luther, and Zwingli are rehabilitated as well-meaning reformers who were goaded into revolt, and Trent is made the real villain of the piece. Trent, as Thomas Molnar says, is regarded by the new ecumenists as having slammed the door on compromise and as representing "the narrow and regrettable victory of an intransigent party over the better-advised but overwhelmed minority of bridge-builders."

But the Council of Trent did not close the door on compromise, for in the terms of the conflict there could be no compromise. What Luther, Calvin, and the rest wanted, as Philip Hughes says in his *Popular History of the Catholic Church*, was "not to reform the Catholic system in which they were bred, but to build up new systems based on their own revolutionary theological theories." Faced with a mortal challenge, the Church had to defend herself; and defend herself she did.

This great Council, the first session of which was held in 1545 and the last in 1563—times when Europe was in a state of political ferment and the Church torn by dissensions and the weakness of unworthy clerics—restated Catholic teaching in reply to the Protestant challenge with clarity, precision, and dogmatic authority. It also drew up regulations for the reform of abuses, codifying and systematizing the plans for the renewal of spiritual life which were the work of a succession of great popes who, with the religious orders which were founded or reformed during these years of crisis, were the spearhead and inspiration of the Catholic Counter-Reformation.

The Emperor, Charles V, who ruled most of western Europe, objected strongly to the Council's dogmatic decrees. Charles, Father Hughes tells us, "feared nothing so much as clear definitions on the doctrinal points in dispute between Catholics and Protestants," and was prepared to compromise on Catholic teaching. But in spite of the Emperor's influence, power, and threats, the Council Fathers stood firm.

The Emperor protested to the last, but his hopes for a rapprochement were dashed. "Once it was made clear that Catholic teaching was divided by an abyss from Protestant theory, there could be no hope of a diplomatic understanding that would allow Catholics and Protestants to be members of the one Church."

Trent closed the door, the new theologians say, pointing out that in the opening chapter of the Vatican II document on Ecumenism it is conceded that at the time of the Reformation "men of both sides were to blame." But the preceding paragraphs of the same document, in spite of their mild and conciliatory wording, are just as forthright as the dogmatic declarations of Trent: Christ promised to Peter that on him He would build His Church; and it is "through the faithful teaching of the gospels by the apostles and their successors—the bishops with Peter's successors at their head—through their administration of the sacraments and through their loving exercise of authority that Jesus Christ wishes His people to increase under the influence of the Holy Spirit." And again: "The Church then, God's only flock, like a standard lifted high for the nations to see, ministers the gospel of truth to all mankind."

The Council's admission that men of both sides were to blame at the time of the Reformation is set in its proper light by Cardinal Bea, whom Pope John appointed head of the Secretariat for Christian Unity set up in 1960. "The Church, it is often said," writes Bea, "bears responsibility for the separation and must in repentance admit its fault openly . . . But we must bear in mind that there is no question here of the whole Church but only of *members* of the Church . . . Dogmatic and moral responsibility must not be confused. The reform decrees of the Council show clearly that the Church, on the practical level of morals, needed reform; but in the field of dogma and doctrine it was still guided by the Holy Spirit and had not gone astray." Then he adds quietly, "It could not."*

The true ecumenists are those who do not minimize the formi-

* *The Unity of Christians*

115

dable difficulties that stand in the way of reunion; the false are those who think in terms of give-and-take discussions—with the giving all on one side. "We should be showing a false love for unity and for our separated brethren," Bea says, "if we allowed them to hope that we will not demand of them anything more than the recognition of 'fundamental articles,' that we no longer ask for acceptance of the dogmatic decrees of Trent or are ready to revise the dogma of the primacy or the infallibility of the Pope. Besides, non-Catholics with clear minds and sound judgement have no such expectations."

Bea counsels mutual respect and understanding between Catholics and Protestants, and stresses the need for continuing prayer, but he returns time and again to fundamentals. "Our adherence to the truth of our faith as contained in the Scriptures and presented to us by the teaching authority of the Church must be *complete* and *unconditional*. No approach to our separated brethren, no work for reunion must weaken that absolute adherence." He is equally clear-sighted and forthright when he speaks of discussions between theologians of both sides. "Their purpose and aim is not, as in a political conference, to work out some compromise on the points at issue—our fidelity to Christ and His teaching would not permit that—but rather to understand the other's point of view and show him our own, in order to see more clearly where there is agreement and where there is not."

But in spite of these cautious words of the Cardinal whom Pope John placed at the head of the Secretariat for the Promotion of Christian Unity, ever since Vatican II theologians like Hans Kung have preached unremittingly that the only thing holding back reunion is the obscurantism of Rome and that all our differences could be ironed out overnight if there were good will on the Catholic side. Their dishonesty and disloyalty has been helped by the popular notion that Christian reunion was the primary objective of Vatican II. The very title Ecumenical Council lends colour

116

to this misconception, since the modern meaning of "ecumenical" is what is common to all Christian churches. But this is not the meaning of the term as Pope John used it, and Cardinal Bea makes this very clear. "The word 'ecumenical,'" he says, "is a very old term in canon law and means only the catholicity or universality of the Church, which of course implies the communion of the individual churches with the See of Peter. So an ecumenical council is one to which all are invited who are in communion with the pope." Admittedly, representatives of the other churches were invited to send observers to the Council, but it would still have been an ecumenical council had they not been asked or had they not accepted.

Ever since the Council, too, the theologians who see reunion in terms of concessions on the Catholic side have insisted that the Church must relax its teaching—or couch it in vague terms which would be acceptable to our separated brethren—on such fundamental issues as transubstantiation and the primacy and infallibility of the pope. Küng, the doyen of this corps, is embarrassed that "superstitions, medieval in form, remain a byword among Protestants,"* and amongst the "superstitions" he mentions pictures, statues, novenas, apparitions, and pilgrimages. All this, and more, is put forward under the plea of "living up to the spirit of Vatican II," although Vatican II specifically condemned "false irenicism through which the purity of Catholic doctrine is jeopardised and its true and indubitable meaning obscured." One cannot help wondering if more harm than good has resulted from the Church's attitude to the rebels, and why the old sanction of excommunication is so seldom invoked. When the disease is mortal, amputation is often the only remedy.

The revolt is open, articulate, and continuous, and the dissentient theologians, whose control of the mass media is notorious,

*Freedom Today

make no secret of their treachery. In March, 1972, thirty-three of them, including Kung and Schillebeeckx, issued a manifesto in which they stated, *inter alia*, that there is "a lack of leadership in the Church," that her credibility has collapsed, and that "no change is to be expected from the top." In the face of this situation, they went on, those who disagree with the Pope and the bishops must not be silent. It was their duty to "show their disagreement publicly and say what they think of the Church and authority," and spontaneous groups were "indispensable" in order to get action on such issues as celibacy and the retention of married priests in their parishes. This manifesto was a direct confrontation with and a call for organised action against the hierarchical Church, and it is difficult to understand why those who signed it were not publicly censured and disciplined. It is still more difficult to understand why they are allowed to continue in office as accredited teachers of the Church.

Nor can we take any comfort from the fact that only thirty-three of the vast army of the Church's theologians signed the manifesto, and that no fewer than twelve were from the theological schools of Nijmegen and Tübigen. For the rot has gone very deep, and in many of the world's seminaries theologians whose opinions are fully in line with those of the signatories and who openly challenge the authority of the Magisterium are still continued in office—and a teaching theologian, it must be remembered, gets his licence to teach from his bishop, who is ultimately responsible for the orthodoxy or otherwise of his teaching. One may well have fears for the priests of tomorrow and the day after when so many seminary professors openly attack the doctrine, discipline, structure, and dogmas of the Church.

Equally alarming is the fact that the new theologians have seen to it that their false teaching has seeped through to the schools, especially in France, the Netherlands, Britain, and the United States. The subversives have laid their plans very carefully and have been alarmingly successful. As Father George Telford, Chair-

118

man of the British Board of Religious Knowledge Inspectors, pointed out in a letter printed in the *Universe* in July, 1970: "The catechetical movement now seems indissolubly wedded to the 'new' theology, and is begetting children who do not seem much at home in the household of the faith." Stressing the seriousness of the situation, Father Telford said that some Catholic teachers had complained to him of what they termed "theological irrelevancies" in the old (pre-reform) religious knowledge programme, and that amongst the issues which they thought of little importance were whether the Resurrection is a historical fact or merely a "spiritual breakthrough," and whether the Eucharist is really Christ's body and blood or merely "transignified bread."

The prototype of the many dangerous catechetical texts now in widespread use was the notorious Dutch Catechism, which a commission of cardinals appointed by Pope Paul found defective on such fundamental points as the Immaculate Conception, the Eucharistic Presence, the Trinity, the infallibility of the pope, and the efficacy of the sacraments. In spite of the cardinals' findings the authors of the Catechism refused to change a single word of it, and the incredible sequel was that, on the pleading of Cardinal Alfrink, the Pope sanctioned the publication of translations provided that the findings of the commission were published as an appendix. "This," a distinguised Dutch theologian commented drily, "is about as helpful as giving our children Luther's Catechism with an appendix of paragraphs from the Catechism of the Council of Trent."* The Dutch Catechism is still used in many catechetical colleges and widely recommended at study courses for Catholic teachers, and it would be carrying charity a bit far to think that it is always studied and criticised in conjunction with the appendix.

In the United States, one of the most articulate of the new

*Rev. P.M. Van der Ploeg, O.P., Professor of Old Testament Studies in the University of Nijmegen

catechetists is Brother Gabriel Moran, who, when Pope Paul issued his *Credo,* made the amazing comment: "His statements don't say anything to me. It's not that they're false. They just don't say anything to me." Since Pope Paul's *Credo* is a summary of basic Catholic truths, it seems improbable, to say the least, that one to whom it says nothing will have anything useful to say to Catholic children or their teachers. Yet Peter de Rosa, one of the avant-garde lecturers who resigned from the staff of Corpus Christi Catechetical Centre, London, when Cardinal Heenan called a disciplinary meeting there,* is on record as saying that Brother Moran had "indicated clearly the path we are to tread if religious education is really to be renewed."

In most of the offbeat textbooks and at most of the indoctrination seminars the New Theology is presented as being no more than the application of modern teaching methods and psychological findings to religious education. The old question-and-answer catechism is derided as arid, uninteresting, and behind the pedagogical times, the implication being that in the past the religious knowledge course consisted of nothing *but* question and answer, whereas as every teacher knows it always included explanation and commentary. But revealed truth does not always lend itself to rational explanation (we can only state the mystery of the Trinity, for instance—we can never explain it), and the old catechisms ensured that every Catholic child was thoroughly drilled in the fundamental truths of religion "which must be known and believed."

The new catechists say that a child should not be taught anything which he cannot understand. (The soul, for instance, is a metaphysical concept, so some of them talk instead of a *me,*

*This meeting—and the protest resignations to which it led—took place in July, 1971. Long before then, however, the Modernist doctrines being taught at the Corpus Christi Centre and disseminated by its graduates had been causing widespread concern amongst parents and teachers.

120

which, as well as making things no easier, makes a sorry mess of the metaphysical concept.) The result is that he is taught very little in some cases.* They say too that he should not be taught truths which might give him nightmares, so hell is out; or which might make him scrupulous, so mortal sin is either ignored or played down.

A. M. Hardie, writing in the famous *Black Paper* on Education, may have exaggerated a little when he said: "At primary school children are taught nothing, and at secondary level they discuss what they have been taught." But he was very near the truth. The new "math can be fun" approach and the notion that the child should discover things for himself wildly distort something which teachers have always known, which is that experiment and discovery have their place in the education of children, and they ignore another basic maxim, which is that some things must be *taught*. These new notions, which are good notions carried to excess, have wrought some havoc in the teaching of the secular subjects, but they have been disastrous in the field of catechetics, where we cannot afford mistakes, and where children must be *told* not only things which they cannot understand but things which they will never understand.

In teaching secular subjects the apostles of the new methodology did not always tamper with the *facts* to be taught, nor did they jettison all of the fundamental skills; children have still to learn how to add and subtract, and long division has not been by-passed simply because some children find it puzzling. In the teaching of religious knowledge, however, the revolution is as much concerned

*At the summer school held in Craiglockhart College of Education, Edinburgh, in August, 1972, one of the nun lecturers said there was no reason why First Communion classes should not be taught that the Mass was a meal—without "confusing" them regarding its sacrificial nature. She also said that the existing four Canons of the Mass were too adult for young children, and that it was permissible for experienced teachers like herself to improvise their own Canons and Collects. The attendance at the summer school, incidentally, included—in addition to priests, religious, and lay folk from Britain, Ireland, Gibralter, and U.S.A.—at least one bishop and one cardinal.

with matter as with method, and it has led to distorted and diluted versions of the deposit of faith and simplifications which amount to perversion. Vagueness has been substituted for the hard-etched lines of theological truth, and the result is such dangerous quarter-truths as (this from a book of teaching aids written by a nun): "The most important sign Jesus has given us is the bread blessed by the priest. This blessed bread is Jesus."

But the mysteries of religion cannot be expressed in baby talk. They must be expressed in clear, unambiguous language or not at all, and there is no good case for peptonizing them. No child can understand the mystery of the Triune God (and neither can any teacher); no toddler can understand how the taste, colour, and form of the bread and wine remain when the substance becomes the body and blood of Christ (and neither did Aquinas); but every properly instructed Catholic child accepts the great mysteries as firmly as Augustine did—and for the same reason. They question everything else, but these they never question, and the strength of their belief does not depend on any teaching methods new or old. There is one motto that should be written in large letters in every Catholic training college and catechetical centre, and it is this: "The child you teach is a baptized Christian, and it is the graces he received at baptism—not your teaching—which enable him to accept unquestioningly the corpus of theological truth which he must know and believe."

If we are not to teach our children about sin, and hell, and the devil for fear of frightening them, we might as well shut the shop (and it would be equally reasonable to say that we should not warn them not to meddle with naked electric wires). There is no reason why we should not—and every reason why we should—put the fear of God into our children, provided that we teach every child too of God's infinite goodness, mercy, and love, and remind him constantly that Christ died for *him* as truly as if he were the only human being who ever lived. Love casts out fear, but the fear of the Lord is the beginning of wisdom, and wisdom cannot begin too early.

The treason of so many theologians and the dangerous catechetical teaching which results from it remind one inevitably of St. Paul's prophecy: "For there shall come a time when they will not endure sound doctrine but, according to their own desires, they will take to themselves teachers, having itching ears, and will indeed turn away their hearing from the truth" (2 Tim: 3,4).

How then fares the Pilgrim Church after its first two thousand years? And why, instead of the triumphal march which we might have expected, have the shadows been constant and the crises continuing?

Much might be said in answer, but the very phrase "the Pilgrim Church" summarises all that can be said. It may be useful, however, to mention three factors stressed by Cardinal Bea in the last chapter of his *Unity of Christians*, which is based on a paper entitled "St. Paul's Vision of the Church in Human History." The first is that the Church is a living organism, and as such subject to the laws of all created life; the second is that its development and health at any given time are influenced by the milieu in which it lives, which may be favourable but is often harmful; the third is the mystery of the Cross.

"The fact that the Church is the Mystical Body of Christ," writes Bea, "and that it lives by His life and that of His divine Spirit, assures us not only that it is indestructible and invincible, but also that it must participate in the Cross of her divine Head. The Church is indeed not the glorified body of Christ but, as it were, a prolongation of the earthly life of Christ the Redeemer. The life of the Church, then, must necessarily be sealed, like the life of Jesus, with the Cross.

"Why then be upset," he concludes, "when across the way of the Church rise mountainous difficulties and obstacles and the Cross seems to grow bigger and weightier?" Why indeed?

123

16
Nothing to
Laugh At

Most of the philosophers and psychologists, and not a few humourists, have tried to rationalize laughter, but in general they have made a sorry fist of it. Stephen Leacock, who could have defined marginal utility or the balance of trade without any trouble, defined laughter as "the kindly contemplation of the incongruities of life." But he had the grace to add: "This is the best definition I know, because I wrote it myself."* Had he spelled out what he meant by "the incongruities of life" he might have done better. He would also have come right up against theology; for an incongruity is something out of kilter, something which does not conform to a pattern; and if life has its incongruities there must be not only some pattern with which they clash but also something in ourselves which enables us to recognize them as clashing—and to take pleasure in the recognition.

And this is where theology comes in; for the incongruity which is the source of much of our laughter is that Man is not, though he often seems to be, the puppet of circumstance. Jokes that stem from the cussedness of things, as so many of our jokes do, are linked with the Christian concept of Man's nature and destiny; and the funny story is not a digression but part of the sermon. The best joke of all is Man himself; and its recurring theme is that

How to Write

125

although he is baulked and thwarted at times by the intransigence of inanimate things like collar studs and broken camshafts, by his own stupidity and the stupidity of those about him, he is bigger than anything that may happen to him. The basic incongruity, one might say, is that walking paradox, Man himself. He is kin to baboon and jellyfish, but he is made in God's likeness and he will live forever. The dogs lick his sores, but his destination is Abraham's bosom.

If we were really stupid, irrevocably and incurably stupid, there would be nothing to laugh at in human stupidity (which is the only kind). But the real meaning of "How stupid of me!" is "How amusing that I should have made a blunder like that!" And even the laughter of born fools would not amuse us did we not know that their foolishness is merely a smudging of the glass of the lantern and that, somewhere within, the light burns as brightly as in the rest of us. (The old Irish called the born fool *duine le Dia* —one who is with God—and the phrase is luminous with meaning. For the born fool is near God already, and not in the same danger as the rest of men of straying away from Him. Moreover, the glass of his lantern will be wiped clean when a new way of knowing replaces the old.)

Laughter, like speech, is a characteristic human coefficient. It is a monopoly of the rational animal, and of necessity a rational activity. We tend to laugh when we see a fat man running after his hat, but there is nothing funny in the spectacle unless you believe—even without adverting to it—in the glory of man; any man; even a very fat man. After all, hats, breezes, and man being given, it is reasonable to assume that once in a while they should proceed along our streets in that order. The funny thing, the incongruous thing is that something as magnificent as a man—any man—should be forced to play second fiddle to something as insignificant as a hat.

To see the point of the joke, or the point of any similar joke,

126

some theology is necessary—perhaps, indeed, all the theology there is. Indeed, it is arguable that a thorough-going rationalist who laughs when he sees a fat man running after his hat or a fat woman caught in a revolving door, has abandoned his principles involuntarily, has taken his stand with those of us who have some notions of spirit and matter, who believe too that a man (even a fat man) belongs to a different order of being than that of hats, jet planes, and monkeys, and that he will outlive the winds that blow about his grave. There is a joke within every joke, and in the last analysis the laugh is on the hat.

"The passion of laughter," says Hobbes, "is nothing but sudden glory arising from the perception of some eminence in ourselves in comparison with the inferiority of others, or of ourselves formerly"; and he goes much nearer the truth than Leacock. But though laughter is a sudden glory arising from a conception of our eminence, the criterion is not the inferiority of others or ourselves formerly. The glory comes rather from a glimpse of our stature as rational beings created in God's image, and when we laugh we salute and acknowledge the superiority of the species to which we belong.

All things other than ourselves are bound inescapably to this or that, but we are *persons,* free to will and love; we can opt for good or evil, and, because of our lineage and destiny, can pray or curse, hope or despair. We are not, ever since the Eden incident, the sort of men we might have been, but we are still trailing our clouds of glory and are not destitute because of Adam's *felix culpa.* At times we seem the fools of circumstance, but we can never be broken on the wheel of chance. We are sons of God, and our present poverty will pass.

It will be objected that laughter is not the monopoly of the Christian, nor does it mark him off from the materialist; but the Christian can offer a rational explanation of laughter, whereas the materialist (who so often, unknown to himself, is drawing on the

127

spiritual investments of his ancestors) is in difficulties at once; for if directed chance or molecular structure governs all our actions there is nothing against which we can measure the unexpected and the incongruous. The materialist creed is that Man, who differs only in degree from the woodlouse, is learning by slow stages, but inexorably, how to dominate his environment. Ultimately, when his growing pains are over (though they have lasted a suspiciously long time) there will be no poverty, no disease, no unhappiness, no hatred. In the meantime, the incongruous has no meaning but tragedy.

Sneering at "pie in the sky," the materialist promises pie here below, but the promise, being postdated and contingent, is poor consolation for the untold millions who must live and die between now and the millenium. Things will come right in the long run, he assures us; but in the long run, as Keynes said, we are all dead; and if the grave marks the end of everything, we shall be very dead indeed.

The materialist counters by saying that sorrow and pain are the price the human race must pay for its perfecting, and that each generation must make sacrifices for the sake of the generations still to come. This amounts to saying that your chances of happiness depend on where you come in the queue. Its heroism is for zealots only. The man who is dying of an incurable disease will take little comfort from the thought that a cure for it may be found when he is dead and gone and that his grandchildren, being luckier than himself, are likely to top the century. Pie in the sky is often derided as a doctrine of alienation, as a myth which turns men from their proper inheritance, the green earth, but at the very least it is more consoling than the promise of pie when we are no longer here to eat it.

If death marks the end of the day, and there is no hereafter, then privation of any kind is an unmitigated evil and the only thing to do is to grab as much happiness as one can before the night falls.

Logically indeed—the premise being given—this is all one *can* do, in view of the way our intellects and our minds work. The intellect judges what is good and the will chooses it—inevitably. A man may deny himself a present good and settle for a future one (dieting today, for instance, so that he may feel better tomorrow), or burn down his house to spite his mother-in-law, but whatever he does his motive is the attainment of what his intellect presents to him as good.

Admittedly, many a man who does not believe in God or a world beyond the grave, far from grabbing as much happiness as he can in this life, sacrifices himself for some political or social cause and dies for it in the end. But he, as surely and inescapably as the rest of us, must choose at every moment of his life what his intellect presents to him as good. The good that he chooses, however, is not his own sacrifices and privations, but their eventual outcome, for suffering is never a good in itself.

But supposing he dies before his ends are achieved? What then? "I shall die happy," he may say, "in the knowledge that the fight will go on and that others will benefit from my sacrifices." One can admire such heroism and altruism, but it seems to contradict the premise that death is the end; for if death is utter annihilation, one does not die happy or unhappy. One may feel happiness or unhappiness when death is imminent, but one brings nothing across the frontier of nothingness, and the good and satisfaction that the intellect promised have no redemption date.

Living—and dying—for some cause which one believes will benefit humanity implies love; and a love which looks forward to its own destruction, to a time when it will no longer be, and to a time also when the object of its love will no longer be, seems a contradiction. If those we love, and we who love them, are alike headed for annihilation, all our love songs will have to be rewritten, and heroism, loyalty, and self-sacrifice are meaningless concepts. If death is not a beginning as well as an end, human suffering is

129

the vindictive dower of irresistible, impersonal forces, and there is no basis for hope, no logical explanation of laughter. If death is the end of the story, we are one with the amoeba, and our laughter has no more meaning than spittle on the lips of fools.

17
Surrender
on Sex

Chastity, says C.S. Lewis, has always been the most unpopular of the Christian virtues, and in the same passage he gives the unequivocal Christian teaching that outside marriage there must be absolute continence. In these days, however, chastity is not only more unpopular than ever, but the permissives no longer regard it as a virtue. Many Christians, too, think that pre-marital and extra-marital sexual relations (which used to be known by harsher names) are permissible in certain cases, whilst the full rigour of the Catholic code, with its ban on contraception, is widely regarded as a set of outmoded ordinances imposed on the laity (those of them, that is, who have not been emancipated by the New Theologians) by a celibate clergy and tending towards mental and physical imbalance.

In the humanist and secular code, morals are restricted to cruelty, social injustice, and bad neighbourliness, and one's attitude to sex is of no more consequence than one's attitude to blood sports, vegetarianism, or changes in the rules of golf. One may do what one likes with one's own body, or with the body of a consenting adult of either sex. Rape and the violation of children (in the physical but not in the moral sense) are out. Everything else goes.

More significant than the decline itself is the attack on traditional morality which has accompanied it. Not so long ago, the Christian code was accepted as determining standards and paid lip service to by those who no longer practised it; now it is derided as an ancient and frustrating superstition from which modern man has freed himself. And the advocates of the new freedom fly the flag openly. "The sophisticate who is no longer shocked by the idea of a homosexual or incestuous couple," wrote Brigid Brophy in a letter to the *New Statesman* in August 1964, "has at least overcome magical thinking; he may be on the point of turning into a reasonable citizen who is shocked that the law should go on interfering with such harmless activities." (In the meantime, of course, the law, having largely freed itself from magical thinking, no longer concerns itself unduly with such harmless activities; but have most of the sophisticates turned into reasonable citizens?) "The collapse of our taboo against theft is not in itself deplorable," Miss Brophy went on (though one would have thought that this is among the few taboos left to us). "Everything depends on whether the taboo is replaced by anarchy or a sound reason (as opposed to the story about the two tablets of stone being handed over on a smoking mountain) against thieving."

"Sound reason" as opposed to the tablets-of-stone syndrome was noticeable here and there in the Longford *Report on Pornography*, some of the contributors to which, whilst being shaken by the mountainous dossier of depravity which it provides, took comfort in the thought that there was no reliable evidence, based on systematic research, that pornography has any adverse effect on conduct—an issue on which, one would think, there is no need for research. Others condemned sexual depravity because it was "depersonalising," anti-social, and often associated with physical cruelty, or simply because they found it revolting and offensive. But if pornography is offensive it must offend against something; and if you leave the tablets of stone out of the reckoning you will have no court to appeal to when someone retorts that what your neighbour does is none of your business and that those who like pornography obviously do not regard it as revolting and offensive.

132

Some of the contributors, however, were more Christian (and more logical) in their approach, notably the Right Rev. Trevor Huddlestone, Anglican Bishop of Stepney, who wrote: " 'Blessed are the pure of heart, for they shall see God.' This is a strictly theological statement, and it raises a fundamental issue which those who believe the Gospel of Christ cannot avoid. Putting it very simply it is the issue of whether chastity is or is not a positive obligation upon those who claim the Christian name."

A simple question this, but it is no longer a rhetorical one, for there are many who still claim the Christian name and yet openly deny the obligation. "Chastity" is an old-fashioned ideal. It went out with the crinoline and Auntie Prue's knee-length bathing costume, and it has no place in the age of the miniskirt. Unchastity is the vogue nowadays, and it is not only practised but preached and flaunted. Sex is good business and the advertiser's best gambit. It sells automobiles, detergents, and foreign holidays. It is blazoned on every hoarding, it dominates screen, stage, and television, and the stock themes of modern fiction are adultery, homosexuality, and sleeping around. Some people wonder whether pornography has any effect on conduct, which is like wondering whether the blight has any effect on the potato crop. Pornography is not a thing apart. Like the cumulative increase in venereal disease and promiscuity, it is a symptom of the blight that is eroding morality the world over.

The staging of *Oh! Calcutta* in London in 1971 marked what the Longford Report described as "a new chapter in the age-old argument about pornography." There were a few protests, a few raised eyebrows, but the critics approved with short-lived reservations and the sex-conditioned public took the new chapter in its stride. One of the protests, however, was remarkable in that it came from A.P.Herbert, who had been a lifelong campaigner for artistic freedom and reasonable liberty for serious writers. "I am sorry to think," wrote Herbert, "that our efforts seem to have

133

ended in the right to represent copulation, veraciously, on the stage." But he might have spared his indignation, for less than a year later the punch line in the newspaper advertisements for a still more daring venture called *The Dirtiest Play in London* was "Makes *Oh! Calcutta* seem like *Little Women*."

"It is a melancholy experience," said Malcolm Muggeridge, speaking at the Edinburgh Festival in 1969, "to see at airports and railway stations everywhere rows of paperbacks all blatantly appealing to our most depraved instincts. In the theatre, things are much the same. Let a collection of yahoos take off their clothes and mouth obscenities and a great breakthrough in dramatic art is announced. I doubt if what pass for art forms have ever been so drenched and impregnated with erotic obsessions, so insanely preoccupied with our animal nature and its appetites, so remote from all other considerations, intellectual, moral, or spiritual, as ours today." Yet all this "sub-standard smut," he said, was "acclaimed as an essential contribution to contemporary letters."

Muggeridge is one of the most trenchant critics of the permissive society, and he knows what its high priests think of him. "I am well aware," he said at Edinburgh, "that to talk in this strain is to invite ridicule as an enemy of youth and progress who is vainly trying to impede the liberation of the human spirit which the birth pill, affluence, and hashish, have made possible."

But the great betrayal of our time is that the new permissiveness is being taught in the schools. In the past, those who lived loosely usually took care that their children did not know of their weaknesses and were brought up in the strict moral code, but this, in the new thinking, is equated with hypocrisy. Sex was cloaked for too long; now it must be brought out into the light of day. It was hidden as something shameful; now it must be revealed as the most important factor in the development of the human personality. The time for lies and fairy tales is gone. The only sin is ignorance, and our children must be given the full facts.

And not just the "facts of life" as they were taught in the old days. Nothing is to be kept back, and it can't be given too soon. Dr. Mary Calderone, Director of the Sex Information and Education Council of the United States (SIECUS), holds that sex instruction should be given to nursery-school children from the age of three, and the SIECUS programmers recommend the joint use of toilets "so as to familiarize kindergarten children with differences in anatomy and physiological processes."

The hard-line stuff comes later. Older students are taught the physiology of sex, including seminal emissions and masturbation, as well as homosexual and other aberrations. "The teachers give blackboard talks, mincing no words, about the formation of sperm, wet dreams, and copulation. During the ensuing class discussions they undertake to answer all questions, however disconcerting, with total candor."*

Seniors have their erotic fantasies aroused by a subject euphemistically labelled "human sexual response," though SIECUS, to give it its due, counsels that this functional briefing should not be "routinely introduced" but should be handled "in private conference." In view of the fact that the topics treated include precoitus fondling, the touching of the breasts and genitals, and other forms of sexual stimulation, the preliminary admonition is understandable. The governing principle, however, is spelt out: "Whatever seems meaningful and exciting to a couple's sexual relationship is acceptable, provided that it does not violate either of their personalities."†

This last qualification is one we hear much of nowadays, but no one has ever explained it satisfactorily. The old "taboos" were clear and explicit, but under the new dispensation there is nothing that would serve as a deterrent to a pupil who has been exposed to

---

*The Individual, Sex, and Society: A Teacher's Handbook. Johns Hopkins University Press, 1969
†Ibid.

pedagogic material which amounts to a detailed "do it yourself" briefing, and which, as someone has said, has the same scientific status as Ovid's *Ars Amoris* whilst lacking its literary merit.

Dr. Kirkendall, the founder of SIECUS, declares that the purpose of sex education is "not to control and suppress sex expression as in the past, but to indicate the immense opportunities for human fulfilment that sexuality offers. It is not moral indoctrination . . ." And Dr. Calderone is even more forthright. "Sex is for fun," she told an audience of New Jersey schoolboys. "It is not something that you turn off like a tap—if you do it is unhealthy." Questioned on pre-marital sex, she pulled out all the stops. "What do you think?" she said. "No one from on high determines this. You determine it. I don't believe that the old 'Thou shalt nots' apply any more."* In view of this plain speaking it is not surprising that in March 1970 a group of English doctors, in a letter criticising the B.B.C. teaching films, should have warned that in the United States sex education had been used as an excuse for introducing hard-core pornography into the schools.

Today's children are not only being taught all there is to know about sex and its aberrations but are being given this information by means of deliberately planned value-free courses—any other kind of teaching, the sex educators say, being a violation of human rights. Thus in the summer of 1971, when Dr. Martin Cole's sex-teaching film *Growing Up* had aroused considerable criticism in Britain, Dr. Cole, far from playing down the film's complete lack of moral content, defended it strongly. "It is the worst form of patronage," he said in an interview given to the *Sunday Telegraph*, "to say 'Make sure you love and respect your partner.' It is selling one's own particular brand of morality—in effect saying 'Don't do it.'" He would be quite happy, he went on, if *Growing Up* were shown in Soho clubs. "After all," he

*The Wanderer, 17 April, 1969

said, "the men in the dirty raincoats are trying to get the sex education they were denied as adolescents."

Oddly enough, in his commentary on the film, Dr. Cole blatantly sells his own particular brand of morality. "Boys and girls," he says, "often have sexual intercourse long before they are ready to have babies. There is nothing wrong in this. However, unless the girl is taking the contraceptive or birth pill, or the boy uses a sheath, she is likely to become pregnant . . . But making love is important to a lot of young people, so be prepared. Never make love without taking precautions."

From the age of mud pies and putty worms, today's children are being deliberately groomed and schooled for the permissive society, and unlike their parents, most of whom had some contact with Christian morality in their formative years, they will have nothing to unlearn. They will take their places easily and naturally in the brave new world; the world which regards contraception as "a sort of polio vaccine designed to deal with the disease of procreation"* and sex as a game without rules; a world in which promiscuity is the accepted ethic (it being the worst form of patronage to say "Make sure you love and respect your partner"); a world in which blue films get bluer and bluer and even the prestigious Sunday papers publish material which would have led to prosecution thirty years ago; a world which accords pornography the status of a legitimate industry supplying a clamant human need; a world in which copulation—real or simulated—may be watched on stage and screen, and in which the sex motif sells everything from central heating to chewing gum. Whether the permissive society will become still more permissive in time (and as things stand it does not even stop short at murder)†is an open

*Dr. Mary Calderone, *Medical-Moral Newsletter,* Feb.-March 1968
†According to the London *Times* (22 May, 1969), an aborted baby lived for eight hours "after it had been taken away in a bag for disposal." And Dr. C.J. Eichhorst, writing in the *Lutheran Standard,* official publication of the American Lutheran Church,

137

question, but now that its recruiting sergeants are at work in our schools the future is anyone's guess.

The deliberate seduction of the young is one of the blackest crimes of our time. "Offences against children" are still indictable crimes, but those who coach children from the age of three and upwards in the mechanics of eroticism go scot free, though they do more damage than the men in the dirty raincoats. If the phrase "violation of personality" has any meaning, this is it; for it is violation with a vengeance.

asked: "How do we respond to the case of the young orderly in a British hospital who quit his job because the 'refuse' he was carrying to the incinerator began to cry?"

138

18

The Treason of
the Clerics

There was a time when most Christian ministers followed the Scriptural tradition and called fornication, adultery, and sexual perversions by their proper names. But this is the age of euphemisms, and plain speaking is out of fashion. Condemnations of sins of the flesh, too, are not as frequent or as fiery as they used to be, and many churchmen even regard them as trivialities with which the Christian conscience need not concern itself unduly. First we had the priests who emphasised that sins of the flesh are not as serious as sins against the Holy Spirit—making it appear that a truth which may be found in the Gospels was a recent theological discovery. And an unwarranted corollary soon follows: the doctrine that where sex is concerned anything is permissible—provided that mutual love and respect are involved. Thus the Rev. H.A. Williams, Fellow and Dean of Trinity College, Cambridge, could say in a letter to the *Church Times* (11 January, 1963): "I believe that goodness consists in generous self-giving and evil in refusal or incapacity to give . . . Where sex outside marriage is the medium of self-giving of this kind, then I would say unhesitatingly that it is not sinful." And in October 1960, when the Anglican Bishop of Woolwich was asked during the notorious *Lady Chatterley* trial if he thought that the book portrayed the life of an immoral woman, he replied: "It portrays the life of a woman in an immoral relationship, in so far as adultery is an immoral relationship."

Christ also had something to say on this question, and He was less accommodating. He pardoned the woman taken in adultery, but He made it clear that He had something to pardon her for.

The Bishop of Woolwich (of whom Malcolm Muggeridge said that he went so far as to "find in poor D.H. Lawrence's sick, perverse sexual ravings an edifying exposition of the Christian sacrament of marriage") and Mr. Williams are not by any means the only Christian spokesmen who have given their blessing to the new thinking on sex, which was approved without noticeable reservations in a short work entitled *Towards a Quaker View of Sex,* published in 1963 by eleven members of the Society of Friends— and which, it is only fair to point out, was severely criticised later by many Quakers. Commenting on what they termed "the increase in transient pre-marital sexual intimacies generally" (fornication has many aliases in these days), they saw in this no reason for alarm nor matter for condemnation, because, they said, "It is fairly common for both young men and women with high standards of general conduct and integrity to have one or two love affairs, involving intercourse, before they find the person they will ultimately marry." But if morality is not something which determines the rightness or wrongness of actions, and is merely something which we observe in or deduce from actions, the question of standards, high or low, does not arise—any more than it does in the rules of grammar, which derive not from immutable precepts but from educated usage.

After this shaky logic, the eleven just men who were groping their way towards a Quaker view of sex (as if this was new terrain which generations of God-fearing Quakers had left unexplored) went on to say that "no one should deplore homosexuality, any more than one should deplore left-handedness." An act, they said, did not appear to them to be sinful simply because of the fact that it was homosexual. "The same criteria appear to us to apply whether a relationship is heterosexual or homosexual." After this,

140

it was not surprising that they should have referred to masturbation as "a natural and reasonable relief," since masturbation is usually a solo performance in which no relational values are involved.

It might have occurred to them that although no one has ever deplored left-handedness, quite a number of people, including a tentmaker named Paul (not to mention the whole dynasty of the Jewish prophets) have deplored homosexuality. And there was once, they might have remembered, a city called Sodom which was dealt with somewhat summarily because its menfolk "had given up natural intercourse to be consumed with passion for each other," and which, as a consequence, had become an abomination in the sight of the Lord.

The theory that everyone is born either a heterosexual or a homosexual is part of the modern ethic, the corollaries being either that God was a little hasty in His dealings with Sodom or that the story of the city which gave its name to a major sin is no more than a biblical myth. But no one is born a homosexual, any more than one is born an alcoholic. Many people are born with a tendency towards becoming one or the other—often a very strong tendency —but the tendency remains latent until it is developed by experience and strengthens into a habit which only heroic self-denial can overcome. Both alcoholism and homosexuality are end results brought about by indulgence, but there is always an interval during which the person concerned is moving towards the compulsive stage.

In the modern ethic, homosexuality is not a vice to be deplored and struggled against, or a shame to be hidden. It is a way of life which may be practised and proclaimed openly without the slightest fear of social ostracism or—in most countries—of the law. There are clubs for homosexuals, dances for homosexuals, and it has been seriously suggested that there should be homosexual "marriages." One social commentator went so far as to say in a

141

letter to the *Listener* (22 June, 1972): "Homosexuality is not only harmless but rather charming, even, in certain cases, impressive— one of the aspects of *homo sapiens* which reveals him as the least limited of animals. Indeed with our present population problems we might well regard it as something to be encouraged."

Now that sex is regarded as a natural appetite completely outside the domain of morals, and when pre-marital intercourse is a commonplace "amongst young men and women with high standards of general conduct and integrity," it is not surprising that contraceptive devices and medicaments should be freely and openly available in most countries. What is surprising is that contraception should be advocated and defended by many who still profess allegiance to the Church that has always condemned it, and that long before *Humanae Vitae* there was ample evidence of the existence of a strong and vocal fifth column of priests and prelates. (Until 1930, we sometimes forget, *all* the Christian churches condemned contraception. The breach occurred at the Lambeth Conference of the Anglican Church.) Moreover, after the promulgation of the encyclical, the dissidents, far from accepting the Pope's (and the Church's) ruling as binding, scouted and derided it. Nor was it a matter of sullen murmurings. It was an open and sustained challenge, and the Redemptorist priest Bernard Haring, in a much publicised article for the American magazine *The Commonweal* in September 1968, called on all in the Church to speak out unequivocally against what he described as "an outmoded understanding of Curial power." Nor was he bird alone. There were Harings everywhere to confuse the laity with talk about the supremacy of conscience (though the issue of conscience applies to contraception in exactly the same way as it applies to all other breaches of the moral law—no one is guilty of sin unless he is aware that he is sinning) and to question the degree of assent due to a decree which, though not involving technical infallibility, was a directive addressed to the entire Church on a

142

moral issue and therefore, like all similar directives, universally binding.

The gymnastics of the clerics who opposed the encyclical were as illogical as they were disedifying and dishonest. "Co-responsibility," for instance, was fathered on the Council, and the impression was created that the Pope, like the chairman of a company, has to have the backing of his fellow directors. The Council, of course, had proclaimed the very opposite—and clearly and emphatically at that. When the pope, it laid down, as supreme shepherd proclaims a doctrine of faith or morals by a definitive act, his definitions "by themselves, and not from the consent of the Church, are justly styled irreformable, since they are pronounced with the assistance of the Holy Spirit . . . and therefore they need no approval of others, nor do they allow an appeal to any other judgment." Moreover (and this makes hay of the "infallibility" quibble) "religious submission of mind and will must be shown in a special way to the authentic Magisterium of the Roman Pontiff, even when he is not speaking *ex cathedra.*" This is not the thunder of Trent, perhaps, but it leaves no room for evasion. The Council could not have said less, and a secondary pupil with a smattering of apologetics (provided, of course, that he had not been brainwashed by the latter-day catechists) could have said as much.

The *periti* and the New Theologians who attacked the encyclical were ably supported—and given inordinate space—by Catholic journals and reviews the world over. They had the help too of the new lay theologians—the journalists who, by virtue of having "covered" the Vatican Council (and occasionally publicised news leaked to them by progressive bishops), were regarded as having tenuous qualifications in theology and awarded such bylines as "Our Religious Correspondent."

Much play was made of the fact that the majority opinion of the Commission set up by the Pope favoured removing the ban on contraception, although the Commission's function was to

143

make a report, not to pass judgment, so that even if its opinion had been unanimous the final verdict and the power to issue it was the Pope's and his only.

The issue of conscience, too, was much to the fore, and it was blatantly misrepresented. Theoretically, a Catholic may come to believe sincerely that he or she is not breaking God's law in using contraceptives, but since a Catholic, in coming to such a decision, must give consideration to the ruling of the Church, it is difficult to see how he or she could claim to be acting according to the dictates of an "informed" conscience. Carrying the doctrine of conscience to extreme lengths, a Catholic who believes in conscience that he must leave the Church has no option but to leave it, but whilst apostasy in good faith is theoretically possible it would seem to verge on a moral impossibility. Such a decision, too, clearly comes from a conscience in error, and it is not easy to see how a person making it could be excused of all responsibility for having allowed his conscience to fall into so murderous an error. Since Vatican II the Church's attitude to deserters, and especially to priest deserters, has been one of the utmost compassion. One wonders, however, if this leaning backwards towards mercy and understanding has been altogether prudent, especially as many of those concerned have made full use of the printing press and the television screen to pose as heroic souls who have seen the light. Compassion for apostates must not blind us to the fact that apostasy is the most horrendous of treasons. This is an issue on which the old Catechism pulled no punches: "The conversion of apostates is so difficult," it said, "because by their apostasy they crucify again the Son of God and make a mockery of Him."

Ironically enough, many of the bitterest and most vocal critics of *Humanae Vitae* were members of religious orders. Moreover, in many cases their superiors made no attempt to discipline them and countenanced a flouting of authority which, had it become general, would have meant the end of all religious orders and

144

which has already wrought havoc in some of them. Some of the most distinguished of the rebels were Jesuits, and in spite of the directive issued by their Father-General, Pedro Arrupe, in July 1968, ordering all members of the Society "to recognise the authority of the encyclical and to see that the faithful respect it," many Jesuits encouraged the faithful to do anything but respect it—a sad departure surely from the spirit of a Society whose members undertake to serve the pope wherever it pleases him to send them and to obey him and their superiors with the unquestioning loyalty of shock troops. The great majority of the Jesuits stood firm —and the same can be said of the Dominicans and the Redemptorists, though each of these orders produced a sizable quota of rebels—but it was the rebels, unfortunately, who made the headlines.

One of the factors which helps to explain the treason of so many prominent clerics, both regular and secular, at the time of Vatican II was the pressures of the permissive society. Going with the current, basking in the publicity which the mass media offered them (for religion had suddenly become news), and conscious of the importance of a good "public image," they persuaded themselves, and soon came to persuade sections of the laity, that since the Church's dogmas could not be reconciled with the needs of twentieth-century man, they must be whittled down in order to bring them more into line with secularist and humanist thinking. Change was in the air, authority was being challenged on every front, "Establishment" had become a dirty word, and if the Church did not curb the power of the Curia and adapt her teaching to the times she stood a poor chance of weathering the storm. Any cleric who preached these views was sure of a welcome in the television studios. It was the day of the rebel.

Another factor was that many of the dissidents were seminary professors and professional theologians, and that in the pre-Council period they had advised confessors who looked to them for

145

guidance that a change in the Church's attitude to contraception was inevitable and that they in their turn could counsel penitents not to worry too much pending the Pope's decision. Then, when the Pope's ruling confounded their prophecies, few of them took the road to Canossa. Instead, they went into open revolt. Quibble succeeded quibble: the rights of conscience; the alleged stranglehold of Curial pressure in the corridors of power; the non-infallible (*sic*) nature of the encyclical; and the suggestion that in going against the majority opinion of the preparatory Commission the Pope had violated the (non-existent) principle of "co-responsibility."

Finally there was the "population explosion" argument, and the warnings—repeated so often that many had come to regard them as founded on incontrovertible scientific facts—that unless population growth was strictly controlled, and contraceptive devices made widely available everywhere, the world would soon be unable to feed—or even to find living space for—its teeming billions. Many of these arguments were soon to be proved unfounded and the "facts" behind them largely fallacious, but the dissident clerics seized on them eagerly as yet another proof that the Church's teaching was behind the times.

19
The Population
Explosion

History has a way of repeating itself. In 1798, when the population of Britain was roughly one-sixth its present figure, Thomas Malthus, a political economist who has been described as the best-abused man of the nineteenth century, prophesied famine in England unless steps were taken to curb the population increase. He recommended late marriages as one way of averting disaster. Exactly a hundred years later, the President of the British Association foretold world famine, his argument being that the supply of wheat could not possibly keep pace with the growth in population, though subsequently the imbalance has gone in the opposite direction and the burning of surplus wheat to keep up the price in the world market is not unknown.

There have always been prophets of doom, and the forebodings of a much earlier one have a distinctly modern ring. "The population is so great," he wrote, "that we are now a burden to the world. There are scarcely enough essentials for us, and our needs have become so great that there is a cry of complaint on the lips of all men." His name was Tertullian, and he lived about 1700 years ago.

One of the claims of those who preach the dangers which uncontrolled growth of population present to the quality of human life is that demography is an exact science and that future population figures can be calculated with reasonable accuracy. Yet the British Registrar General's office, which predicted some years ago

147

that the population of England and Wales would reach 70 million by the end of the century, has since adjusted its estimate to 58 million—a margin of error which it is difficult to reconcile with any claim to scientific accuracy. (Incidentally, the higher figure is still often quoted by the alarmists.) Among the wilder statements that have been made about the population explosion is that in the foreseeable future the earth will be so crowded that there will not be standing room for its people. How wide of the mark this prophecy is has been shown by Dr. Colin Clark, one-time Director of the Agricultural Economics Research Institute at Oxford, who has pointed out that if all the people in the world were transported to the United States the density of population there would be about 300 per square kilometre. And this, it may be added, is approximately the present density of population in the Netherlands, one of the world's great food-exporting countries.*

Standing room being assured, what about food? As far back as 1954, Sir Dudley Stamp, speaking at the World Population Conference, said that the world was cultivating only about a third of its potentially cultivable land—and most if it very badly; and since then Arthur McCormack has estimated that with increased capital expenditure and modern farming methods, and in view of possible agricultural developments in very cold regions—prospects for which are much brighter than they were in 1954—the cultivable land of the world could be increased six-fold.† Moreover, Dr. Colin Clark believes that with adequate use of fertilizers and planned crop rotation the world could support over ten times its present population, and this without any further improvements in agricultural technology.** It is worth remembering too that since the discovery of such "miracle cereals" as Mexican short-stemmed wheat and Philippine IRB rice, production figures per acre have

*Quoted in *Christian Order*, March 1972
† *The Population Problem*
** *The Population Problem in Perspective*

148

risen dramatically, so that Mexico has become a wheat exporter and both Pakistan and the Philippines now export rice.

Admittedly there is severe malnutrition and even famine at times in parts of India and Africa, but it does not by any means follow that these regions are incapable of feeding their people. In much of Africa, for example, only a small proportion of the potentially cultivable land is under crops; and in India, where enormous numbers of sacred rats and sacred cows are maintained, the yield of rice per acre is roughly a quarter of what it is in Japan. The developed countries, as successive popes have recommended, should do everything possible to help the undeveloped countries, and although they have already done much they could still do more; but to say that there are too many people in India, Africa, or anywhere else is to dodge the real issue, for "too many" waits on "How much?" and the fact is that the food-producing possibilities of many of the world's undeveloped countries have scarcely been scratched. Meanwhile, in a world which, we are told, has not enough food to feed its people, Australia has too much butter, Brazil too much coffee, and Denmark too much bacon.

The history of the discreditable part played by the UN World Food and Agricultural Organization (FAO) in the population explosion scare, which it may be said to have inaugurated, is told by Dr. Clark in his *Starvation or Plenty?*. First came a statement by Lord Boyd-Orr, Director-General of FAO, to the effect that "a lifetime of malnutrition and actual hunger is the lot of at least two-thirds of mankind" (*Scientific American*, New York, August 1950). When this estimate was shown by a distinguished food research expert to be based not only on inaccurate statistics but also on an arithmetical error in handling them, the FAO reduced its figure from two-thirds to a half, but without giving any supporting evidence or even revealing its standards of malnutrition. Nevertheless this "starving world" announcement was widely accepted, and amongst those who used it in advocating urgent

149

measures for population control and family planning were President Kennedy and Prince Philip (who went so far as to suggest that contraceptive chemicals might be added to public water supplies).

Eventually it transpired that the FAO figure for the minimum calorie intake per head per day (2300) was based on the *actual* figures for France and Britain—countries whose food consumption can scarcely be regarded as marking the starvation boundary; and an Australian anthropologist has pointed out that if the FAO figure has any validity, then in Japan, despite its prosperity and high standard of living, the majority of the population must be starving. Dr. Clark cites the example of China, where in the early 1960s the calorie consumption per head per day was only 1600. Admittedly a calorie consumption as low as this indicates hunger and hardship, but as Dr. Clark comments wryly: "If the FAO figure of 2300 for minimum calorie requirements is correct, most of the population of China must be dead by now."

The misleading standards of the World Food and Agriculture Organization, which Dr. Clark has so effectively ridiculed, may have sparked the population explosion scare, but the chain reaction was brought about by books like Dr. Paul R. Ehrlich's *The Population Bomb*, which has gone through edition after edition (in paperback, too, so that it reached the mass markets) since its publication early in 1968. Ehrlich backs up the unsubstantiated FAO assertion with some wild statements of his own, and the cover of his book bears the grim legend: "While you are reading these words, four people will have died from starvation, most of them children." Assuming that this passage can be read in four seconds, the implication is that one person dies from starvation every second, or about 32 million every year. Since the total number of deaths in the world when Ehrlich's book was written was in the region of 54 million, the deaths from starvation would seem to account for 59%.

150

This is a horrendous figure. It makes one think, and it has forced some people, scenting flagrant distortion, to do a little investigating. No separate figures are available for world deaths from starvation, but an American commentator, using the statistics given in the UN Demographic Yearbook for 1969, has pointed out that the total deaths from diseases which could be attributed to nutritional deficiencies (including parasitic diseases and cirrhosis of the liver) were under a million.* The error factor in Ehrlich's statement is therefore about 32, which means simply that his estimate is 32 times too big. In fairness it must be admitted that if the reading time for his cover legend is extended to five seconds (which should get even the finger-pointers in) the error factor is reduced to 25.6, but whilst this would involve a slight change in the charge sheet it would scarcely give grounds for acquittal.

It is undeniable that malnutrition is rife in many areas of the world, and that there is urgent need in these regions for improved methods of cultivation, as well as for massive help from the developed countries whilst the changes are being effected. But the contention that population growth is in danger of outstripping the world's potential food production and that disaster is inevitable unless births are drastically reduced everywhere is based on statistics that are demonstrably false, as well as on predictions that have no scientific basis.

*Michael Lawrence, *Triumph* Magazine, February 1971

20
Humanae Mortis

Strangely enough, hysteria about the "population explosion" was largely confined to the western democracies, in most of which there was no explosion whatever, and in many of which the graph had begun to level out. The undeveloped countries were seen as the danger, and they were to be saved from themselves by advisers whose job would be, not to popularize the new high-yield cereals, or to point out the folly of protecting grain-consuming vermin in countries where periodic famine is endemic, but to spread the good news of contraception. Children, not rats, were to be thinned out.

In the developed countries themselves, the gospel was to be preached to the poor and the "culturally disadvantaged" and—as a matter of urgency—to people on public relief. Many of those who campaigned for the spread of contraception were moved by sincere humanitarian motives, but it would be naive to believe that altruism was the dominant factor in the new thinking. The poor were to be indoctrinated, ostensibly for their own sake, but in reality because it was feared that they tended to crowd out those who, in the popular phrase, had never had it so good. Left to themselves, it was said, the poor "bred like sows." They polluted the environment as dangerously as toxic fumes and factory waste, and they would have to be trained in—and if necessary have imposed upon them—techniques which would enable them to

153

copulate as freely as their betters without increasing their already exorbitant claims on the public purse.

The Church's condemnation of contraception was branded as a frustrating and outmoded ruling imposed by desiccated and obscurantist prelates who had no knowledge of and were not in the least concerned about the day-to-day problems of married people. The truth is, however, that knowledge and concern set the tone for *Humanae Vitae*, in which Pope Paul made it quite clear that he appreciated the difficulties of married people and realised that keeping the moral law often entails heroic sacrifices. Indeed he went further, saying that for many the Church's teaching must seem hard or even impossible, that like all things truly for man's good it needs firm resolution and great effort, and that without God's grace it *would* be impossible.

Far from opposing responsible parenthood and family planning, the Church recognises the need for it. It approves the use of the sterile period, and in *Humanae Vitae* the Pope exhorts doctors to give their attention to investigating methods of determining its duration more accurately. The Church's approval of the sterile period method of regulating births, however, has occasioned even more blistering criticism than her condemnation of contraception. The "safe" period, its critics say, is far from safe. It is no better than Vatican roulette, and is a niggling concession which imposes unnatural abstinence. Moreover, the Church's approval of it is a dishonest quibble aimed at the avoidance of open revolt. If contraception is wrong, then use of the sterile period is equally wrong, since both have a common aim and in each case the intention is the same.

But the distinction drawn by the Church between contraception, properly so called, and the use of the sterile period (which, incidentally, is the only method of birth control which involves a measure of self-control), is utterly logical, since there is all the difference in the world between taking advantage of a natural

154

phenomenon and using appliances or drugs which stultify or impede a natural process. Coition retains its procreative *character* when it occurs during the sterile period, but it loses this character, and so is condemned, when any action is taken before, during, or after the marriage act to make the transmission of life impossible.

But the Church's condemnation of contraception (which did not originate with Pope Paul, who simply reasserted it) must be distinguished from any logical defence which may be made of it. The ruling is infallible; the arguments are not, and though all Catholics are bound by the ruling, any Catholic is free to disagree with the arguments. In *Humanae Vitae*, Pope Paul says to priests: "We are speaking especially to you who teach moral theology— to expound the Church's teaching with regard to marriage in its entirety and with complete frankness. In the performance of your ministry you must be the first to give an example of that sincere obedience, inward as well as outward, which is due to the Magisterium of the Church. For, as you know, the Pastors of the Church enjoy a special light of the Holy Spirit in teaching the truth. *And this, rather than the arguments they put forward, is why you are bound to such obedience.*" (Italics added.)

A harsh ruling, this on contraception? Not harsh, but hard; so hard that, as Pope Paul says, without God's grace it would be impossible. This puts the responsibility—and the authority— where they belong, for Pope Paul said too that he was speaking by virtue of the mandate entrusted to him by Christ. "We have no wish," he said also, "to pass over in silence the difficulties, at times very great, which beset the lives of Christian married couples. For them, as indeed for every one of us, 'the gate is narrow and the way is hard, that leads to life.' " Keeping the moral law is always hard, and it is hard for everyone; otherwise there would be no merit in it. If the Church's condemnation of contraception seems harsh, what of the ruling that outside marriage there must be absolute continence?

155

Contraception is not just a technique. It is a way of thinking, an attitude to life—and death. It is not surprising then that in all countries where contraception is widely practised the number of abortions increases yearly. Abortion, indeed, is the logical corollary of contraception. If human life is not sacred, the point at which it is destroyed is not relevant, and abortion is a defence in depth; if the enemy is not stopped at the first onset he may be halted by the reserves.

Ever since the publication of *Humanae Vitae* a number of Catholic theologians have misled and confused the laity by maintaining that whilst abortion is all wrong, contraception in certain circumstances is all right; which is on a par with saying that abortion is sometimes right and infanticide always wrong. The spokesmen of the permissive society are more logical. They hold that if contraception fails, the pulsating life in the womb may be stilled as soon as its presence is detected. Some of them advise, however—as a concession to some unstated moral code—that the killing should be done before the foetus has been too long in tenancy. Occupation for twenty weeks or so is regarded as conferring squatter's rights and remission of sentence, and one churchman (not a Catholic) is on record as saying that no question of morality can possibly be involved in removing "a piece of foetal jelly" from the womb. It is ironic to remember that it was as a piece of foetal jelly that he himself began his distinguished career, and that he was as much a *person* then as when he sat for his master's ticket.

It was contraception that opened the sluice gates, and once it was legalised and made respectable there was no way of answering those who clamoured for abortion. (Not that there were always separate lobbies. In France, for instance, those who campaigned in favour of contraception, saying that abortion was abhorrent to them, formed themselves into an abortion lobby as soon as the first objective was won.) And the doctors were the first to capitulate.

156

Just as the permissive society and the promiscuousness which it preached introduced an element of amateur competition into the ancient trade of harlotry, so furtive back-street rooms gave way to state-supported hospital wards in which murder could be done in aseptic conditions and with less danger to the life of the accomplice.

Descriptions of abortions rarely find their way into the daily papers, most of which miss no opportunity of publicising the lurid details of indictable murders, but whether this delicacy is due to consideration for the public stomach or the public conscience is an open question. Certainly any such description would bear out the statement of Pastor Dietrich Bonhoeffer (who is widely quoted in contexts other than this) that "abortion is murder." Bonhoeffer was speaking as a theologian, but one does not need to be a theologian—or a doctor for that matter—to realise that abortion *is* murder. The techniques speak for themselves, and here, for those with strong stomachs, are some extracts from a paper read by Dr. P.H.Dunn, Fellow of the Royal College of Gynaecologists and Obstetricians:

"The surgeon must work by touch alone; he gives a tug; a tiny arm comes away; then other portions of the body. The head is always difficult; the skull gets crushed; the eyeballs protrude. All the time, the bleeding is profuse. When the abortion is complete the problem of the disposal of the remains has to be faced. Incineration is the favourite method. . . .

"She [the mother] has a general anaesthetic. The womb is incised, and the baby is lifted out. It makes weak movements of the arms and legs and tries to breathe. Sometimes it manages a few pathetic cries, like a kitten. Then, after a few minutes, it dies an asphyxial death and lies coldly in a stainless steel bowl. . . .

"A large needle is inserted through the abdomen into the womb and a strong solution of salt or glucose is injected. The baby can be left to make a few convulsive movements, and in a few minutes

157

it dies. In about twenty-four hours, labour starts, and the already disintegrating body is delivered."*

In the face of evidence like this, it is clear that abortion is predated infanticide. A human person—an Abe Lincoln, a Florence Nightingale, a Michelangelo—is deliberately done to death. To contend otherwise is to dodge the facts. The abortion of a living foetus, irrespective of at what particular stage of development the pregnancy is "terminated" (that aseptic and conscience-dulling word), is deliberate murder carried out at the behest of a mother who is willing to sacrifice the life within her womb rather than burden the world with another "unwanted child."

Descriptions of contraceptive methods are much less harrowing than this and they will not affront the squeamish much more than, say, a description of the removal of a cyst from an eyelid, but squeamishness is no sure guide to the morality of an action. Many so-called contraceptives are really abortifacients, since they either destroy the fertilized—and living—ovum directly or ensure its destruction by preventing it from nidating. Moreover, all contraceptive techniques (even sterilisation) are at least potentially abortive, since they deprive the sexual act of its normal character by providing conditions which rule out procreation; and a man who tosses a bomb into a house is no less guilty if by pure chance no one happens to be in it at the time.

The contraceptionists, who talk glibly about their concern for the quality of human life, have no regard for its sanctity, and it is not surprising that euthanasia should be the next step in the programme of the permissive society. If we may snuff out new life early without qualms of conscience, we are equally entitled to take steps to ensure that those who are so old that they have become a burden to themselves and to society should be snuffed out when they have outstayed their welcome and become a strain on our

*Quoted in a pamphlet published by the Lamp Society, 1970.

resources—preferably, though not necessarily, with their own consent, and in these twilight hours the question of consent will be misty on one side at least. Indeed, if the quality of human life is what matters, the case for euthanasia is open and shut, for people are living longer nowadays, the number of pensioners is increasing, and there are limits to what wage-and-salary earners can provide for their support without disrupting the national economy. (Ironically enough, the problem of senilization is aggravated by contraception, which cuts down the number of contributors and tends to worsen the imbalance.)

Contraception, it is worth repeating, is an attitude to life—and death; and the title of Pope Paul's historic encyclical, *Humanae Vitae,* summarizes the moral issue involved. What we are concerned with is not *primarily* sexual pleasure, marital rights, and the need for family planning (though all these are relevant and important factors) but human life: not the quality of human life, but human life as such. Either it is sacred, God-given, and inviolable, or it is not; and both abortion and euthanasia are logical corollaries of that death-wish that we call contraception.

2 1
Decline and Fall

Christopher Dawson, writing in 1936, envisaged the rise of a western society "which would acknowledge no hierarchy of values, no intellectual authority, and no social or religious tradition" but would live "solely for the moment in a welter of pure sensation."* Dawson's central thesis was that religion is the cohesive force which gives unity to every civilization and provides a focus for every culture, and he saw this emerging society, which is now approaching full term, as one which must lead inevitably to social disintegration.

In no sphere of conduct has the rejection of social and religious tradition been more evident in recent years than in that of sexual *mores*, and it is interesting that Dr. J. D. Unwin, writing some years before Dawson, concluded from a study of many past civilisations that sexual licence is the sign and source of the decay of every culture.† Unwin's theory has met with criticism as well as support, but it is worth attention as being based on a completely objective study, since, as a committed rationalist he had no Christian axe to grind. Sexual immorality is not the only or the most pernicious kind of immorality, but the sixth and ninth, which used to be known as the difficult commandments, might also be regarded as

*Progress and Religion
† Sex and Culture

161

the shoring ones, since when they go by the board the rest tend to topple like ninepins. "You cannot," as Dag Hammerskjöld said once in a different context, "play with the animal in you without becoming wholly animal."

We must distinguish, however, between a society in which sexual licence is practised by many people, or even by most people, though the moral code which condemns it is still recognised, and a society in which sexual licence is not only the accepted practise but the accepted ethic, in which the code that condemns it is regarded as a medieval superstition, and in which all ideas of moral sanctions are deliberately eroded from the minds of the young. The first may be a Christian society; but the second is certainly a post-Christian society. A nation or an age which opts for sexual licence as the satisfaction of a natural right puts the *homo naturalis* in place of the *homo religiosus*, with the result that, sooner or later, it adds new dimensions to its initial revolt and opts for licence on all fronts.

And this is what is coming to pass in our own time, in an age when, as C.S.Lewis says, the sexual impulse has been placed in a position of "preposterous privilege," and the "right to happiness" is cited to defend what in many cases is little better than the morality of the farmyard and to condone behaviour which in any other department of conduct would be rated as evil and unjust. Moreover, the revolt spills over, for morality cannot be departmentalized; and once we come to believe that we are entitled to indulge our sexual urges when and how we please, we come to regard self-gratification as the sole rule of conduct and become arbiters in our own cause. Virtue is one, and morality is a package deal. What is involved is the acceptance—or rejection—of an external authority. It is all or nothing, and there can be no picking or choosing. Saying that you are free to accept some of the clauses and reject others is like saying you are willing to obey on Mondays, Tuesdays, and Wednesdays provided you are free for the rest of the week.

162

In the "welter of pure sensation" that Dawson foresaw, straight sex gives way to aberrations, and as the appetite cloys the unending search for fresh stimulation leads many to hard drugs. Drug-taking offers the hedonist an escape from the astringent world of reality, and it is significant perhaps that his excursions into this never-never land where no writ runs but his own should be known as "trips." In the end this dream world of erotic fantasy and paranoiac delusion becomes more real to him—because of the heightened sensations which it offers—than the world of hard fact. The drug addict is society's cripple, but all who follow the will-o'-the-wisp of sensation have a touch of his moral deformity, since in time, and to a greater or less degree, they lose the power to go against their own inclinations and come to resent all that stands —or that seems to stand—between them and self-gratification. They equate conformity with surrender, and regard obedience to anything or anybody as the ultimate degradation. Family ties, parental authority, the laws of Church and state—all these, as well as teachers and policemen (who in the new idiom are known as "pigs"), are lumped together under the all-embracing title of the Establishment and fused into a single tyranny.

One of the axioms of the revolt against the Establishment is that senility begins at about thirty-five and that the young must refashion the social order of which their fathers have made such an unholy mess. But there is no question of adapting or improving. The cure is to tear down and destroy. Nor can we who are long in the tooth comfort ourselves with the fiction that campus riots, sit-ins, "marches" for anything and everything, attacks on university offices and civic buildings, and the burning of draft cards and examination records are no more than signs of a youthful ebullience that will pass in due course; for all these have a philosophy behind them, and it is the philosophy of revolution.

Lacking the stability and sense of civic responsibility which even the *pietas* of pagan Rome might have given them, the pampered waifs of the permissive society are ready-made recruits for the New

163

Left. Their only philosophy is some vague notion that wrongs will be set right when all those who possess authority are forced to share it with—or even cede it to—those over whom they exercise it, and they fail to see that what is at stake is not the powers of proctors, policemen, or senior citizens but Christian civilisation and the democratic notions that derive from it. Challenging authority, they support a philosophy that is rigidly and brutally authoritarian; demanding freedom, they endorse a system which tramples on freedom and sees the ordinary citizen as having no rights other than those granted to him by the leaders of the oligarchy; marshalled in clamorous "fronts" they demand peace in faraway places and indict imperialism and colonialism as the obstacles to brotherly love—though the old imperialist powers have dismantled their empires piece by piece, and most of the colonies and vassal states left in the world are behind the Iron Curtain. Campaigning for a more just distribution of wealth, they refuse to see that even as an economic theory Marxism has proved such a sorry failure that in order to prevent famine wheat has to be imported into the great grain-growing districts of eastern Europe, and they cling hard to faith when the shortage of consumer goods in Russia, Czechoslovakia, Hungary, and Poland is put down to sabotage or explained away as a growing pain which will be eased shortly by yet another Five Year Plan. Spoiled children of the affluent society, their myopia blinds them to the facts of recent history, and they have never suffered the disillusionment of men like Milovan Djilas, whose bitter experience in his native Yugoslavia forced him to concede that Communism in action suffers from all the economic ills which it had stigmatised as the sins of capitalism.

Dr. Unwin's assertion that unrestricted sexual freedom is the sign and source of the decay of a civilisation has been criticised as a rash generalization, but it finds a supporter in Lenin, who boasted—and it was no idle threat—"We will seduce the youth

164

of the west by sex and drugs." But though the Russians encourage and connive at sexual licence in the west (and the Chinese make sure that hard drugs will always be in plentiful supply), they were quick to stamp it out at home, and they soon eradicate it in each satellite country which comes under their spreading power mantle. They see it as part of the softening-up process which paves the way for the takeover and as producing a spiritual void which their own propaganda may help to fill, but it has been abandoned as part of the long-term plan because experience has proved that it militates against production in field and factory. So we have the ironic situation that whilst the Christian teaching on sex is largely flouted in the west it is being followed to some extent for expediency's sake by the hardheaded atheists of the Kremlin. It might be said too that Communism has given a partial assent to Dawson's thesis that religion is the cohesive force which gives unity to every civilisation, since all its high priests from Marx and Lenin to Stalin and Khrushchev have preached time and time again that Christianity is the cohesive force behind the western civilisation they are minded to destroy, and Engels' "declaration of unremitting war against religion" is still honoured to the letter.

Is our western civilisation doomed—the civilisation to which Christianity for so long gave direction and purpose, gave ends as distinct from means? Certainly the prophets of doom have spoken clearly. Oswald Spengler, ten years before Dawson, saw in it "all the characteristic stigma of decay";* and Jean de Fabriques, writing in 1967, could say: "We are now living out the final moments of a religious and sacral civilization which is becoming a lay civilization."† But a civilisation does not simply decay and leave the premises untenanted. The barbarian is at the gates long before its demise, and the weakness within is accompanied by the challenge

* *The Decline of the West*
† *Christianity and Civilizations*

without. Unless it rehabilitates its moral fibre, our new secular civilisation, cut off from its roots and with neither philosophy nor creed, will be no match for a Communism which, although basically and essentially irreligious, has all the inspiration and driving force of a religion.

Meanwhile there is cold comfort in the thought of the United Nations and of "peaceful co-existence," which, as Douglas Hyde says, is "a euphemism for a state of affairs which the Communists believe they will be able to use in order to subvert one country of the free world after another."* The tactics of Communism change from time to time, but the final aim is unchanged, and it was the smiling Khrushchev who said in Berlin in 1963: "We will bury capitalism, but the burial will be achieved by the workers of each country; they will bury their own capitalists."

The Communist theory of the dialectic is that thesis, antithesis, and synthesis determine the march of history. Thus feudalism, because of its own internal contradictions, leads inevitably to capitalism, and capitalism in its turn, and again because of its own weaknesses, will lead inevitably to Communism. The sequence is as predictable as successive chemical reactions. To the thoroughgoing Marxist, the ultimate triumph of Communism in the world is as certain as tomorrow's sunrise, and this belief was put into words by a man of our own time when he said: "I believe in the philosophy of thesis, antithesis, and synthesis. From its present antithesis, I believe that the world is moving on to a new synthesis."† It was not a very original confession of faith, but it was certainly a notable one; and what makes it notable is that it came from U Thant, who held the not unimportant post of Secretary General of the United Nations. How "neutral" then was U Thant? And how impotent was the United Nations when, in November

*The Peaceful Assault
†Newsweek, Nov. 13, 1961

166

1956, because the Communists had the veto in its Security Council, it stood idle when Khrushchev used savage Mongolian troops to crush the Hungarian Freedom Fighters?

The west might still be saved if it realised the need to stem its own moral collapse and the strength of the Communist threat to which its moral weakness exposes it, and hopes on both fronts might be brighter if the Church had stood firm. But the Church has not stood firm, and it no longer speaks with one voice. We have on the one hand the churchmen who favour concessions to the permissive society on such fundamental issues as divorce, contraception, and abortion, and on the other the priests and prelates who, looking to their public image, see revolution (and they mean revolution) as the only cure for the world's economic ills. Pope after pope has condemned Marxism, yet Marxism is now recommended as a subject for serious study in seminaries, not with a view to equipping future priests to meet its arguments but with the naive object of Christianising something which of its very nature is basically anti-Christian and anti-God. We are told that we must come to terms with Marxism and see what is good in it, which is like exhorting us to come to terms with cancer and see what is good in that.

Admittedly there are signs of a Christian counter-attack, but it is weak and inarticulate and its spokesmen get a poor showing from the mass media, in whose corridors of power the permissives and the fellow-travellers are strongly entrenched. There are many too who are afraid to speak, and who, it would seem, have lost their nerve. If they recover it soon, we may avert disaster. If not, our descendants will have to rebuild a shattered world when civilisation makes a fresh start.

22
On Death

Most of us speak about death at times—speak of it with a spuriously philosophic air of accepting the inevitable, but our thinking seldom reaches the point of hurt. "It will happen to us all sooner or later," we say on the day of a funeral (the day of all days on which whiskey and tobacco taste their best), and then we add the unspoken corollary that in our own case it will be so much later that there is no point in bothering about it now. We are also given to dodging our fear of death by an affected horror of senility, saying "I'd hate to live to be ninety"—though the answer to this piece of hypocrisy is "Come back, son, when you're well in the eighties and we'll have another chat about it." It is the other fellow who is liable to go at any minute. We ourselves will die peacefully in our beds when we are old and tired and beyond caring.

It might be thought that the committed Christian should need no such lenitives, since he believes that the happiness of this world is as nothing compared with the glory to come. But things don't work out that way. The Christian, as much as anyone else—and perhaps even more than anyone else—is in love with the green earth which, in spite of the pains and frustrations it brings him at times, is the only heaven he knows. And there is nothing pagan in our love of life. It is the way God made us—and it is part of our debt to Him.

There are no atheists in rubber dinghies, it has been said; but

I am not so sure. I cannot help thinking, too, that if I were hurtling earthwards in a disabled plane I should probably feel more scared than the atheist beside me; for he would be thinking only of the split second of the bump and I would be worrying about what comes after it.

I knew one man who was so scared by the thought of dying that he never went to a funeral, though there was one funeral, in the end, that he couldn't dodge attending. The saints went to the other extreme. They thought of death often, and some of them kept skulls in their rooms to remind them—which to modern man seems macabre and revolting. But perhaps not so macabre after all, since every man keeps a skull under his hat and each one of us is a walking skeleton; complete with eye sockets, hip bones, and scapulae; padded for the moment, but fated to be laid bare in time; for dissection is as complete in the grave as in the anatomy class.

Fear of death, for the Christian, is fear of the judgment. But why, God's infinite mercy being granted, should we fear the judgment? Surely all our offences will be pardoned in the end by the most compassionate of Judges. It would be comforting to rely on this hope, but it would be presumption to rely on it completely, since the same merciful Judge, when He walked the earth, spoke in language which strikes a chill into the heart. If your right eye offends, pluck it out; and for some at least there will be weeping and gnashing of teeth.

But will every son of Adam, as soon as the breath leaves him, be plunged at once into eternal happiness or eternal misery? The Church has never said that (and "at once," for that matter, is a concept rooted in time rather than in eternity), for it speaks of a purgatory where souls can be scoured in a cleansing fire, a merciful reformatory in which suffering will be mixed with hope and a postdated happiness. I like to think too—though with no theological backing to justify such thinking—that there will be a chance for a final declaration of loyalty—or disloyalty. Undoubtedly the choice will depend largely on how one has lived, but I like to think

170

that there will be an opportunity for choosing, for voting for Christ or against Him, and that sentence will not be passed unless final obstinacy on the part of the defendant makes no other verdict possible.

Why then all the pother? If we are all to have an equal chance at the end (though I have not said quite that), what does it matter how we live? The answer to that is that all through our lives we are growing towards God or away from Him, that we are always becoming more like what He wants us to be or tending back towards nothingness. Christ promised a reward, but He laid down specific conditions and preached a way of life that involved continual self-denial, a way of life which would seem folly to the wise. He left us through His Church a moral code which had not only to be followed but also to be preached and defended, and the price of its defence was often ignominy and death. A life of self-gratification is not—and cannot be—a spiritual life. We must choose between God and self. As Paul says, we must run the race and fight the good fight if we are to win the crown; and Paul, like Alan Breck, was a bonnie fighter.

Hell has been scrubbed out by some modern theologians, and reduced by others to a mere figure of speech, but if there is no hell in the sense of a place of eternal suffering then Christ's passion and death are meaningless folly. The Son of God died to save us, and to save us from something; and that something, assuredly, must be a reality of unimaginable horror. But its real horror is the annihilating sense of being cut off forever from the love and friendship of God, and an eternal remorse and hatred so all-embracing that it involves and is even centred in hatred of the self.

Death is a punishment, and as a merited punishment it is a cleansing and salutary thing. It is the last submission, the final expiation. "Do not go gentle into that good night," wrote Dylan Thomas, "but rage, rage against the dying of the light." But we *must* go gentle, and rage at the end is the ultimate blasphemy.

Robert Southwell's advice to his ageing father was at once

171

kinder and more realistic. (But then Southwell was a saint as well as a poet.) "And having so many harbingers of death to premonish you of your end," he said, "how can you but prepare for so dreadful a stranger . . . Be not you therefore of those that begin not to live until they are ready to die; and then, after a foe's deserts, come to crave of God a friend's entertainment . . . Wherefore, good Sir, make no longer delay; being so near the breaking-up of your mortal house, take time before extremity to satisfy God's justice . . . For surely, wheresoever the tree falleth there shall it be; whether it be to the south or north—heaven or hell—and such sap as it bringeth, such fruit shall it bear."

Harshness? Pity and love, rather, affection and passionate pleading. While the breath is in us there is always time, but we are dealing with a thief that strikes in the night, and we dare not put things on the long finger.

Death, willingly accepted, is a modified martyrdom on easy terms. The Honours men lay their head on the block; the rest of us get a test that is tempered to our weakness, and all that is asked of us is to accept the inevitable without complaint or grumbling. We must die whether or no, but God pays us the tremendous compliment of inviting our assent and leaving us free to withhold it if we will. The choice is ours. We can resist to the end and rage, rage against the dying of the light; or we can go gentle into that last good night, trusting in His mercy and submitting to His will. And everything depends on our response, for it is the last chance we shall have on this earth and we shall soon be beyond choosing.

172

23

One Christ,

Loving Himself

Christ's human nature was not something that He assumed until the drama of His earthly life was over and then shed as a snake sheds its skin. He was God from the beginning that was not a beginning, and man only from the time of His conception—but the period of His adoption was forever. He sits at the right hand of the Father, but He retains His created body and His created soul.

Christ's humanity is the saving of us, and when we pray "through Jesus Christ, thy Son our Lord," we should advert to the meaning of a tailpiece without which our prayers might seem too audacious for utterance. Our claim to a hearing is based on kinship, since we are sons of God by adoption, and we lean on the words "thy" and "our" to remind Him, like importunate suitors, that we who have nothing have something in common with Him who has everything.

In Christ we are raised up; in Christ the dichotomy of our wretchedness and our glory is resolved. He partakes eternally of our humanity, and our prayer and hope is that we shall share eternally in His divinity.

We shall be absorbed in Christ, but not as drops of water are absorbed in the ocean; for in being absorbed we shall not lose our separate identities (which are so precious to Him). Christ as God remains inaccessible, yet in some way that passes our comprehension we shall all share in the divine nature and receive a gift so unthinkable that had we not Christ's word for it we might well doubt that even God could give it.

And our sharing in the divine nature has already begun. Christ is the vine and we are the branches. The supernatural life that He gives us flows from Him and through us without ceasing, and as members of His Mystical Body we are linked with Him and with each other to form an integral whole in which each part remains separate and distinct.

We can think if we like of some complex molecular structure in which immense numbers of atoms are riveted together, but the analogy will not get us very far; for atoms of the same substance are identical, and we are not identical. We must not think of the Mystical Body as a formula expressing the repetition of approximately identical terms. It is a progression, undoubtedly, but it is composed of terms whose disparity is their very *raison d'être*. For we are not fashioned from a common mould, nor is our number —the final, ultimate number of us when the roll call is complete —an arbitrary choice of the Creator. He has made us thus and thus and in a predetermined number, so that the bulked and final accounting will have meaning and significance, with each one of us making a distinct and separate and necessary contribution. Ours is not an infinite series, but when it is complete it will reflect— though in an imperfect and finite way—the infinite majesty of God.

Each of us is unique, because each of us possesses a rational, immortal soul, directly created by God and a masterpiece in its own right; and our uniqueness conditions our individual reactions to and our individual ideas of everything from tripe to chamber music. I know my neighbour, and he knows me, but neither of us knows the other as he really is, nor can either of us do more than guess at the other's reaction to a shared experience. Each of us lives in a closed fortress, and neither drugs nor conditioning techniques

174

can breach its defences. No one is there to keep us company except the omnipotent, omnipresent God. Even the angels are barred.

We try to make contact with those about us, but words and gestures are effective only up to a point. The inability to know fully and to be known fully, to give fully and to receive fully, has always cast a shadow on human affection, and even in the best love poetry there is a note of frustration. There is only one who knows each one of us as he really is, and that is the Man Above.

In the next world we shall share in this knowledge, seeing ourselves and those about us in the measure that God permits. In seeing God, and in knowing and loving Him, we shall see what makes us different one from another, and how we are all—in the mass and as individuals—linked with Him and loved by Him. We shall also see ourselves for the first time, for we shall see ourselves in Him, and it is only in Him that we are really meaningful. He must increase and we must decrease, but our decrease will not be a shrinking nor a diminution. In Christ, our pilgrimage ended, we shall reach our full stature. Our selfhood will be complete and intelligible; and in the end, as Augustine says, there will only be one Christ, loving Himself.